DATING FOR WOMEN

A MODERN WOMAN DATING GUIDE

JOANNA WELLS

CONTENTS

INTRODUCTION

I couldn't believe my luck! I was sitting in front of a stunning man, way out of my league. He was Australia personified—tall, tanned, so well built. I don't know what came over me. I was in a supermarket when I saw him. I had been so determined to change my life that I had woken up a confidence I had never experienced before. Although I was sure he was going to say no, perhaps he just enjoyed the shock on my face when he said yes.

The luck ended there! Bless him, as my gran would have said: "He was at the front of the queue when God gave out looks, but he was hanging around the end of the queue when He was handing out brains". The end result was another failed date and a wasted evening.

In my twenties, I was too young and polite to call it a day without allowing the date to play out. I spent many nights sitting in front of a date who talked endlessly about football, his ex, or himself. Maybe I was still a little too naive and optimistic. Maybe I was so desperate to find my true love that I couldn't just walk away.

The biggest problem is that although today I look back in fondness on this one date (and all of my perceived 'failed dates'), at the time, it was heart-breaking. It took all my will to put myself out there, all my courage, and it just felt like another failed date in the line of many. I felt that this was my problem and that it was something I was to blame for.

Dear gran continued with her words of wisdom: "You have to kiss a lot of frogs before you find your prince". She was so right, although others have put it more delicately:

"Better to put your heart on the line, risk everything and walk away with nothing than play it safe. Love is a lot of things, but 'safe' isn't one of them."

— MANDY HALE

Yes, it's true, and it is better to have loved and lost than never to have loved at all. But I started to question whether the people behind these quotations had gone through the same experiences I had. Or had they lost one love and got it right the second time?

On the one hand, I was lucky to have called upon the last strands of confidence I had to date. Still, more often than not, the apparent failure of my dating left my confidence shattered. Each time it became harder to put myself out there. Other people don't feel they can even get as far as going on a date, and I have been there too.

Every date I went on I started to question myself. Am I good enough for this person? Were my clothes suitable? What if I wasn't funny enough or smart enough? I would literally get in the shower feeling that this date was going to be different and by the time I had got out, I had convinced myself that I should just cancel. It was becoming harder and harder to be optimistic about each new date.

Then I started to feel frustrated with myself. My negativity was probably causing me to miss out on the one. I was punishing myself for something that hadn't happened yet and inevitably setting myself up for failure. There was a massive amount of negativity around every aspect of dating.

Mentally, we tell ourselves that this date will be different, and we will find Mr Right. Though we all know that we are only half convinced of this and whether it's our emotional baggage or whether we attract the wrong guy, we go back to square one. Like me, you may have even felt that you weren't even close to square one.

Then there is that friend. You know who she is! You love her to bits and wouldn't change her for the world, but you can't help envying her ability to flirt and have fun. She has this self-confidence that you can never imagine yourself having. Trying to be more like her feels false and leads to anxiety.

We are going to look at dating in a modern, practical way—one that allows you to explore who you are and understand exactly what you want in a relationship. Regardless of our age, career, or past issues that may still haunt us, we will discover tools for a variety of objectives.

There are plenty of factors that can cause setbacks in the world of dating, some are psychological, others may be social. It is easy to turn those factors into self-doubt. We start to believe that we will never find true love. In reality, it might only take a change in perspective or learning to let go of past relationships so that we can move forward.

There is no one approach to dating—that would undoubtedly make life a little boring. Some people have a high-powered career or another demanding lifestyle, around which a love life must somehow be arranged. Others may have lost the love of their lives and have no idea how to venture back into the dating world.

The most important thing is that you are learning techniques that you can use in your life without wasting any more time on men who don't deserve you or men who aren't looking for the same as you are. And equally important, we are going to have fun doing it.

At the same time, I want this book to be unique, so I am not going to tell you that I know exactly how you feel. I wasn't with you on each of your dates; I didn't live with you through your relationships. What I can promise is that like you, I have been on more failed dates than I wish to count. I was single for all of my twenties and the best part of my thirties. Everyone around me seemed to be getting it right, while I was just feeling more and more lonely.

What made the difference was when I began learning more about psychology. The subject intrigued me, and it became practically the only thing on my internet search history—ok, that and the dating websites! I then saw changes in myself once I started practising mindfulness, something else that we will work on. The combination of psychology and mindfulness with a decent dash of dating experience is what has led me to where we are today.

The techniques I used to do work—my husband is proof of this. Even better, he is a good husband who I truly love. It's only right that now, I enthusiastically share what I have learnt so that you can find the happiness that you deserve. Let's begin by going back to the beginning and discovering your true self.

1

WHO ARE YOU AND WHAT ARE YOU LOOKING FOR?

L ooking back on my dating experiences is like looking back at your cringe-worthy photos from the past. Things spring to mind like "Did I really do that?". There are some typical dates that we have all been through. The other person talked too much about themselves, or worse, their ex. They spent their entire time checking their phone. They were rude to the waiter...

My favourite disaster was the date who knew everything. He was a political expert, a fitness freak, he had obviously travelled to more countries than I had, spoke more languages, you name it. Perhaps it was nerves. Maybe he was trying to make a good first impression, but all it did was make me feel stupid and then angry. When he started telling me how I should be doing my job, I gave up. This was the date that made me feel like the dating game was just exhausting.

Although you might be keen to jump straight to the chapter full of successful dating tips, to get the process right, you need to start from the beginning. For me, this was to take a look at all of my dates and start to work out why they had gone so wrong. Rather than making it a pity party, I decided that this would be best over a bottle of wine, or two, and in the company of a good friend who had patiently listened to all of my disasters.

With a pen and paper, we listed each date, the activity, the good and the bad, and then the ugly. From there, we looked at how I felt about each date, my expectations for each one and what I could have done differently. And then we asked what on Earth led me to say yes to some of them for a second date. These questions were the beginning of the process of working out my purpose for dating.

WHAT DO WE ACTUALLY KNOW ABOUT DATING?

By this point in our lives, probably a lot. But I'm thinking about our late teens, early twenties, or when we first started dating. Since there is no class taught alongside Maths and Science, all we know is what society tells us, what we see in films and on TV, words of wisdom from friends and family.

The problem is, this is still all based on how women should be. Even if the twenty-first century, it is often assumed that women should be more passive in a heterosexual relationship and even in the workplace. A man who goes out for what he wants is ambitious and determined. Women who do the same are rarely praised and are more likely to be insulted. Have you ever had someone try to push your personality back in its little box with comments like, "You'll never get a husband like that"?

Women will often feel guilty for looking for a relationship that will actually make them happy. It is better to do what the crowd is doing, not to rock the boat and step out of society's expectations. Find yourself a good man! As if the most important thing is that he is good rather than whether you actually like him. This is the advice we receive. I'm determined to tell my daughter to have a relationship full of mutual love and respect.

BEGIN BY REDISCOVERING YOURSELF

Can you honestly remember who you were before you started dating? When you were positive and you had dreams? There was a time when you could look at yourself and instead of looking at how men saw you, you saw yourself. You had hobbies that you enjoyed, types of films you loved, food you wanted to try.

As the dates and relationships go past, you begin to change. This might not be intentional: you eat at restaurants that your partner likes or prepare meals that are their favourites. You sit through the entire James Bond collection instead of binge-watching Grey's Anatomy. These things might seem small, but each one has a small impact on you.

You may have had dominant partners who told you what to wear and how to act. You may have grown to fear expressing who you really are because of the potential consequences.

I decided that I needed a clean slate. I didn't want to forget my past, because I felt there was plenty to learn from it, but if I wanted to be happy in a relationship, I needed to be happy with myself. We need to appreciate self-awareness.

I began by redefining my goals for that period of my life. I asked where I wanted to see myself in one year, three years and five years. I was brutally honest with myself and made sure I focused on what I wanted to achieve, rather than what was expected of me. I remembered what I used to love doing before others seemed to organise my time for me. I thought about the passions that I had left behind.

By doing the same, you will be able to identify the things in your life that you need and want for you. You can work on improving how you see yourself and on becoming more confident about who you are. You may realise that you want to learn more, change your career, or travel. You may want to upgrade your wardrobe, exercise more—the possibilities are endless—but the first step is to think about yourself and not to feel guilty about doing so. I believe it is your right as a human being to be happy.

Interestingly enough, when I looked at what would make me happy in the following one, three, and five years, it wasn't a husband. And from here, I learnt that I had been looking for the wrong thing in my dates and relationships.

HOW TO START DATING WITH A PURPOSE

Maybe one of the principal reasons that our dates continuously go wrong is that our purpose is wrong for the stage of our lives. I am a huge Disney fan, but the traditional princesses did our generation no favours. Snow White had one date, singing with the animals in the forest, when she met her true love. Bella from

Beauty and the Beast had it a little rougher, learning that love is more than looks, but still, she only had to turn down one arrogant French man to live happily ever after.

Because we feel that we need to find a man to get married, settle down and have children, this is often the purpose of our dates. That's an awful lot of pressure for someone you may have swiped yes to or at most had a phone call with. What we think we need is not always what we want.

For some, dating is the first step to creating a life with someone. For others, they want a fun partner who they can experience new things with. Then there are people who just want to have sex. Imagine—a woman who just wants to have sex! Surely only men can do this? Whether it's love, sex, or marriage, the purpose of your date is going to have a large impact on your dating experience.

IDENTIFYING THE PURPOSE OF YOUR DATES

This is not a prolonged exercise; you don't need to continue with your list of what you have learnt from past dates unless you want to. The following points are things to think about while you are driving to work or exercising, but do think about them sometime before you go on your next date.

1. Set your own boundaries

If you are unaware of your boundaries, people will continue to cross them and this will lead you to feel upset, angry, and negative about yourself. What do you like to do in your free time? How would you feel if your partner doesn't enjoy the same things? How do you feel when someone disrespects your values or beliefs? Are you willing to let it slide or can you express how this makes you feel?

Setting boundaries doesn't make you pushy or dominating. It is a set of rules that you like to live by. Your date doesn't need to have the same boundaries as you do. You can follow football and he can follow rugby, but you both need to respect the other person's beliefs and interests. He needs to know what you are comfortable with and vice versa.

2. What are your absolute noes?

If there is one thing I will never accept in a relationship, it is racism. I used to be quite timid and hardly ever make a scene, least not on a date. One of my favourite failed dates that I am actually quite proud of was when the guy I was with turned around and started talking about Chinese people. Naturally, in his narrow mind, they all ate dogs and had funny eyes. I tried to show my discomfort, but he just kept going on. Speechless, I stood up and walked out.

Know what you will not tolerate, no matter what the purpose of your date is. This will save you quite a bit of time, especially on second dates you know aren't going to work.

3. Do you have the same goals in life?

If you are on the first or second date, you probably aren't going to take out your list of goals and start asking if they see themselves getting married and having children. But if your purpose is long term commitment, it is essential to know these things early on. If your date sees themselves on annual cruises and island-hopping while you see yourself with a big green garden and two kids running around, your goals are not in line.

If you have had a relationship with someone who has different goals, you may have learnt this the hard way. The first year or so might be wonderful bliss. You ignore the fact that they don't want children, because you are sure they will change. How would you feel if they expected you to give up on your goals?

. . .

4. Know what you want and need in a relationship

It's hard for women to talk about what we want as we are conditioned to put the needs of others first. While we aren't allowed to be too strong, we don't want to be weak either, but there is a balance and your partner should appreciate that you have needs too.

Some people will want to be able to explore their sexuality, travel, to feel safe, to have a level of financial security, to feel equal. Others may feel that physical affection is more necessary for them, or that their partner gets on well with their family. Try to get a list of about ten things. If you can't see your date or even your partner fulfilling these needs, then you might need to consider moving on.

5. Look at the significant relationships from your childhood

More often than not, we carry our parents' problems with us into our adulthood. The good and bad aspects of your parents' relationship can provide insight into the mistakes you are making. Talking to groups about their childhood experiences highlighted for me one of the most significant psychological issues that women can have relates to their father's behaviour. A cheating dad leaves an all-too-harsh image of men on a young girl's mind. This can stay with us until we learn how to heal from it. Every man we meet we naturally assume is going to behave like our father.

It doesn't have to be negative. There are many things that we can learn from our parents' loving relationship that we would like to see in our own. Couples in their fifties who still show each other affection are demonstrating something that I hope to achieve.

6. Create a vision board

Now that you know what the purpose of your dates is, you can create a vision board. This is great for creative people who prefer not to write lists. Find images, words and short phrases, cut them out and create a collage. At the top of your vision board, include the things that are absolutely essential, in the middle, place those things that you can compromise on, and at the bottom, add the things that you will not put up with.

WHAT DOES A HEALTHY RELATIONSHIP LOOK LIKE?

There is no such thing as a perfect relationship. If you have asked your friends or family members what makes a good relationship, they might start listing all of the amazing things their partners do. Every relationship at some point will have its ups and downs; it's about as guaranteed as taxes. Those who tell you how wonderful their partner is might be trying to convince themselves more than they are you.

Here are some qualities of a good relationship that both you and your partner should feel:

- Respect of each other's intelligence, opinions, and beliefs
- Trust and honesty
- Support when times are hard
- Equality in all areas
- Individual identities
- A sense of humour

And then there is the great attractiveness debate. If we say that attractiveness is important, we are accused of being shallow. But let's be honest, if there wasn't some kind of physical attraction, what would make you want to date them in the first place? It is very true that looks are not everything and when you get to know a person, there are plenty of things to fall in love with. In the world of dating, I feel it is important that there is an initial spark.

There are other cases when this isn't so. We have heard of best friends throughout school and university who stay together forever. It can also happen when you aren't necessarily looking for romance. You can meet a person and find them fascinating and an attraction can develop from there. In these situations, love and an attraction developed from a friendship and with time to get to know the other person. It's not quite the same as seeing someone in a bar and asking if they would like a drink.

The need for attraction in a relationship is debatable, especially when you consider physical and mental attraction. It's up to you to decide how much or even if it is a priority for you.

HOW DO YOU KNOW WHEN IT IS THE RIGHT TIME TO MOVE ON?

You think you have met the love of your life and your first few years are a whirlwind of romance. In your head, your wedding is planned, and you have named your children. Then you discover that there is another woman. Your entire centre of gravity shifts as you know that your world will never be the same again.

The first time this happened to me, he apologised so much and took me away for a weekend and proposed. Well, this just had to be a sign that he had changed, right? Wrong! It was probably three and five women later that I found the courage to leave. At this point, I had no confidence, no willpower and no passion.

People might hear that story and scream, "Why? You should have left after the first woman!" This is true; however, it's never that simple. Ending a relationship can make you feel like you have failed. There is also the fear that you will never find anybody else, even the fear of telling your family and seeing their disappointment.

This can be similar to those who are in an abusive relationship. You and I both know that you should leave, but the thought of starting over is almost scarier than what you face each day. You don't want to feel like you have failed, you know he loves you really, and it's not all bad. All I can say is that there is support out there for you. It doesn't have to be your friends and family: it can be community groups or counsellors. I kid you not, jump on my Facebook Group and we will come up with a plan together. You know that you need to leave but you have to be ready, and we will be here!

Now that you have reconsidered your needs and what you want from a relationship, you need to analyse your current situation and make some decisions. As mentioned before, if there are more than four or five things on your list that you can't see working, it might point to an unhealthy relationship.

Before calling it a day, you could speak to your partner and see if there are things you could change so that you both can be happier. At least then, if things don't change, you can put your hand on your heart and say you tried everything.

Ending a relationship is never going to be easy. Allow yourself some time to work through your emotions. Take some time to explore who you are. Talk to people and get help if you feel like you need it. Start with baby steps; don't feel like you need to go and conquer the world straight away. In those early days, even taking a shower can require an effort, but each baby step will help you to start getting back on your feet. Don't be too hard on yourself if the recovery takes longer than you hoped, and remember that everyone works through things at a different pace. It probably won't be long until you start to feel a sense of freedom and that a weight has been lifted from your shoulders.

HOW TO KNOW WHEN YOU ARE READY TO START DATING AGAIN

The word 'ready' has a powerful punch in the world of dating and relationships. Have you ever heard someone tell you they aren't ready for a relationship? Did you fake the smile and say, "totally agree, me neither", just to go home and cross off another potential?

Did you know that before the 1950s, the term "ready for a relationship" didn't exist? Before this period, marriage was what made people grow up and become an adult. You didn't need to figure anything out before you felt ready for a relationship.

As times changed and women began to look for a career and their own source of income, they began to prioritise things differently. It wasn't until the `80s that the concept of readiness really began to make a significant presence and then in the `00s, we started to use it perhaps a little too much. It is true that in many cases, we don't feel ready. However, those using it as an excuse to let someone down gently has led to the expression "I'm not ready for a relationship" becoming a bit of a cliché.

Unfortunately, there isn't a handy timeline that can help us to decide when it's the right time to start dating. For some people it might be a couple of months, others need more than a year to feel like they can face going on a date. Age or experience plays no role in this. It will more likely depend on your previous relationships.

If you can relate to the situations below, it probably means you are ready to join the dating scene again.

- **You aren't scared of getting hurt**- you know that your quest for true love will have some challenges, but you also know that finding your perfect partner will be worth it.

- **You embrace change**- each and every cell in the human body dies and is replaced every seven to ten years. Nothing is meant to stay the same. Accepting this means you are ready to embrace the changes that a relationship goes through.

- **You don't see commitment as a restriction**- rather than looking at commitment as marriage, you view it as an emotional promise to someone you want to share your life with.

- **You have an amazing sense of energy and freedom**- instead of trying to act as if you fit in or how you think you should, you are able to be yourself and this is a great motivation.

- **You have learnt from your past relationships**- you hold no bitterness or regret. You understand that everything has happened for a reason and you now know exactly what you want in life because of your experiences.

On the other hand, these are some signs could warn you that you aren't ready to start dating just yet:

- You have been on some dates and seem to be attracting the wrong type of person.

- You don't feel complete being alone, you feel that you are missing something in your life.
- You see a partner as a project, someone who needs to be saved from their problems.
- You are dedicating more time on finding a partner than you are on your own passions.
- When you are in a social setting, you act differently to how you normally would, probably unintentionally, but you feel that the real you is not enough.

You may find that you will agree more strongly with some of the signs pointing to whether you are ready or not. It is possible that you can clearly see why your past relationships went wrong, but you still have some regrets. Or maybe you don't feel alone but you would be happier with some company.

If this sounds true, it might be wiser to spend at least a few weeks learning more about yourself and becoming happier with who you are before you start dating. Rushing the process can lead to more bad dates, and let's face it, we have probably had enough of that for now!

WHY IS IT GOOD TO DATE?

How do you know what your favourite alcoholic drink is? When I was twenty, I liked Diamond White—a strong white cider (I'm feeling old now because I don't think you can even buy that anymore). Now, nothing beats working hard all day, achieving all I had to do and enjoying a glass of Chardonnay. Not a Riesling, or a Pinot Gris, or Sauvignon Blanc—a Chardonnay! I know that I don't want a whiskey or a beer or a sweet wine because I have tried them, and I don't like them.

This, my female friends, is why dating is good. Choose anything you know you like, skirts over trousers, mountains over the beach. You know what you like because you have gained experience. Dating has to be seen in the same light.

It goes back to society's view of dating and women. Too many dates and we get accused of being all sorts of things. A man gets a pat on the back and a "get in there, another date!" Women get the horrified "another date?"

When you know what your purpose is for dating, it becomes a lot easier to see that each date is not a failure. If you want to enjoy a full social life, dating is a great way to do new things with new people. If you are looking for a serious commitment, dating allows you to explore your options rather than limiting yourself to a few potential suitors.

Dating gives you a chance to learn more about yourself. You might think that there are boring and interesting qualities about you. Your ex may never have laughed at your favourite joke, but your date might. By looking at how you feel before and after the date, you have the ideal time for self-reflection.

The more dates you go on, the easier it becomes to clarify your idea of what is important to you in a relationship. You may have thought that table manners weren't a big issue until you sat in front of a date chewing their food for the whole restaurant to see. Instead of seeing dating as a chance to find the love of your life, use it as a way to clarify what type of partner you want.

Once the pressure to find the love of your life is removed, you will notice that dating is actually quite fun. There are a lot of laughs to be had, a lot of blunders, and a lot of fond memories to create. I hope I'm not alone here, but I got a guy's name wrong once, ok, actually twice. Luckily my hands were shaking so much I think he put it down to nerves and forgave me, obviously not enough for a second date! We live, we laugh, we learn.

If you are reading this book, it's because you know that you need a fresh start when it comes to dating. We aren't going to erase our past, but we have to let go of the hurt, forgive ourselves and our ex-partners so that we can genuinely start with a clean slate.

You also need to change your perspective. First, it's time to see dating as fun again, and second, you have to know that it is ok for women to date and explore what they want from their lives. From here on, there is no more guilt or shame; there is a search for happiness and enjoying yourself, knowing that you have found your purpose in dating.

There will still be some mistakes that we tend to make when dating. So before choosing our outfit for the next date, let's cover some of these errors so that we know not to make them going forward.

2

COMMON MISTAKES THAT ARE KILLING YOUR DATING GAME

I did promise that we would have some fun while exploring dating and this is definitely one area that we can fondly smile about and even cringe. It might have been us or it could have been our dates, but mistakes have been made. I will start by confessing one of biggest mistakes before sharing some funny moments that people have shared with me.

I suppose, looking back now, it is safe to say that from nineteen to twenty-one I wasn't ready for a relationship. I had a habit of losing my dates. We would go out for dinner, things seemed fine, maybe we would go for a drink or two at a club after. I remember seeing a friend and getting distracted or I would go to the bar, but essentially, I didn't tell my date that I was going somewhere and that I would be back. In my mind, they spent all night searching for me. The truth is they probably just left.

Becky told me about a date who kept looking out of the restaurant window. He popped outside a couple of times and she assumed it was to smoke. Actually, his mum was waiting in the car.

Paige was impressed with her date's muscular body and assumed he worked out. They actually talked a little bit about their fitness routines and when he talked about working out in the yard, she assumed he meant the garden. She assumed the black thing around his ankle was a weight. The yard was actually in prison and the ankle weight was a tracking bracelet.

Penny was really pleased when she went on a first date with a guy who was genuinely very funny. Not just a little giggle but a full belly chuckle that leaves your eyes watering. While driving home, she was laughing so much that she said: "I love you". It was the comfortable 'I love you' that you say to your friend or your sister, but it still caused a bit of a weird atmosphere.

I won't even begin to mention all of the stories where people went out on a date and discovered that they were related.

Lisa also thought that things were going well. Her date leaned across and ran his fingers through her hair. She saw this as a good sign and went in for the kiss. He pulled back quicker than a lightning bolt. He was only trying to remove a bit of fluff from her hair.

Part of moving on is about learning from our mistakes so that we don't do them again. It's difficult not to think that maybe that mistake cost you more than you want to imagine. But there is little point in dwelling on this and it is better to smile at the memories. I could wonder if one of the dates I managed to lose in my free-spirited years would have turned out to be the father of my children, but they didn't, so I am happy looking back and having a laugh.

If you have been dating for a while but don't feel that it has been very successful, it could be that mistakes are being made. If you are ready to join the dating scene again, it will be worth learning about some of the most common dating mistakes and how to avoid them.

NOT BEING TRUE TO YOURSELF

We talked about this in the first chapter—the idea that we should behave a certain way because it's what is expected of us. This is truer in the first few dates. We think our date is looking for a particular person and we act like this unreal person rather than ourselves. Unfortunately, this is likely to be because of low self-esteem and lack of confidence. We might act like someone we aren't because we don't feel good enough about the real us.

This is most noticeable when ordering at a restaurant. How many times have you looked at the big juicy steak or the surf 'n' turf but ordered a salad and mineral water? That is what women do right? Men want a woman who can eat, plus they don't want their girlfriend stealing their food later on because they didn't eat enough! By not ordering what you want, you aren't showing your true self. At some point, your date is going to have to learn about the real you or you are going to have to sacrifice steak for a salad for your entire relationship.

The salad is just one example, it could flow into what you wear, how you express yourself, and your likes and dislikes. During your first few dates, you create a character that isn't you. The longer this lasts, the harder it becomes to make the necessary changes. It's also not fair on your partner. You have made the assumption that they wouldn't like you for who you are, not even giving them a chance. As the relationship goes on, the false pretences will only cause you both pain.

NOT TALKING ABOUT EXPECTATIONS AND INTERESTS

It may have been that you have dated without fully understanding your expectations, the boundaries that you have and the purpose of your dating. A common mistake we also make is to not talk about our interests or expectations. Let's tackle these two separately.

There is a right way and a wrong way to talk about expectations early on in dates. The wrong way includes brushing them under the rug or becoming all matter of fact. You're not Mary Poppins, listing your expectations of a child. The word 'expectations' may even be a little strong for first dates, so stick to talking about your hopes and dreams, what you are aiming for. There is nothing wrong with a woman having goals and directions and it isn't something that men should fear. The first few dates are like laying the foundations. If you don't like men holding the door open for you, now is the time to set this straight politely.

Similarly, you might be more comfortable agreeing with similar interests that you have with your date. The more you ask each other about what you both like or don't like, the sooner you start to discover how compatible you are. Having different tastes in films or music can be a case of "opposites attract" and a good opportunity to expand your music collections. Nevertheless, it's the early dates that allow you to discover if there is something too different that you won't be able to overcome.

COMPARING RELATIONSHIPS

I used to do this all the time. I would look at friends and wish that my relationship could be more like theirs. I wanted my boyfriend to show more affection, hold my hand when we went for a walk. Secretly, I was a bit of a hopeless romantic but never told anyone this, which explains why I tend to buy my own flowers! We also fall into the trap of looking at celebrities' relationships and how perfect they seem to be. Nobody really knows what goes on behind closed doors. Comparisons raise our expectations to unreal standards and more often than not, lead to disappointment.

It's also quite natural for us to compare dates or new relationships with an ex. Imagine if a man on a second date bought me flowers and I said, "My ex would never have done that". It sounds like a compliment but really, nobody likes being compared. Your date may simply feel like you are still caught up on your ex.

What you have with this person is unique: never before have these two individuals spent time together, and this should be given respect, it should be looked at with fresh eyes and not measured against other people. Be careful that your comparisons don't set your new relationship up for failure.

YOU FEAR IT'S TOO GOOD TO BE TRUE

Every once in a while, there will be that perfect date and the butterflies in your stomach just won't slow down. The excitement is a rush and amazingly, the second date goes just as well, and the third. You have done it. You have met your prince (or princess) charming. Everything is perfect. But wait a minute, this is not your life! Nothing is ever perfect, so this must be too good to be true.

When our brain starts telling us that it's too good to be true, our subconscious can begin to sabotage our good thing. You have little control over this, so don't kick yourself too much. It normally stems from a fear of getting hurt or what is known as cognitive dissonance —when your behaviour and your beliefs contradict each other. The rational part of you doesn't agree with the rush of chemistry you are experiencing with your perfect partner.

Pay close attention to the initial rush of chemistry, but don't shy away from it. Enjoy this stage, as it is an essential part of dating, and it is part of what makes it so much fun. That being said, don't let it blind you from seeing someone's flaws, and when you do see these flaws, it doesn't mean that this person isn't perfect for you.

FALLING IN LOVE TOO QUICKLY

How many times have I kicked myself for doing this? It doesn't matter if I told myself it wouldn't happen again or if I said that this time, I would take things slower, even friends would ask after the third date if I was head over heels. I used to phone my very first boyfriend's home every twenty minutes to see if he was back yet. His parents must have thought I was crazy. The word 'clingy' is the only one that comes to mind!

Love at first sight. Is it possible? Is it blinkin' Disney getting our hopes up again? It's only a personal point of view, but I prefer to call it 'lust at first sight'. Everything is new, pheromones are whizzing around faster than Lewis Hamilton and we are whisked away in a flow of chemicals that might make us feel like we are in love.

"Lust shouts. Love whispers. Only the heart knows the difference."

— JAN HURST-NICHOLSON

Again, this is a time that should be enjoyed but for what it is. Assuming you are in love so early can have two negative consequences. Frist, you risk not giving each other the necessary time to get to know each other. Second, when you fall in love so quickly, you are essentially taking yourself off the dating scene and you could miss out on other exciting experiences.

Being clingy shows that you need a man to complete you and that you aren't comfortable being by yourself. If your purpose of dating is a long-term commitment, both of you must be allowed to continue with your individual lives. You don't want someone constantly texting you while you are with your friends or family, and neither do they.

REMAINING DISTANT

Of course, you want to come off as cool and give the impression that you aren't sitting next to the phone waiting for him. You need to have your own life still and make plans. But because we have been fed so much rubbish advice about keeping him interested and playing hard to get, we actually think this works!

In the `70s, various studies were carried out with regards to playing it hard to get and the conclusions pointed towards there being no greater attraction when women told a man that she was too busy. Just think if you said you were too busy, and your dream date didn't ask you out again.

We are also still under the impression that we should wait for the man to make the first move, whether that's an invitation for the next date, or even the first kiss. Maybe your date is hoping for you to make the first move, perhaps this is what they are looking for in a relationship and it is what you want to do, but neither of you goes for it, because you are worried about what others will think.

It goes back to being true to ourselves and if something feels right at the time you should do it. If you are busy, offer an alternative, so that your partner doesn't think you are playing games. Speaking of which...

PLAYING GAMES

Dating mind-games come in all shapes and sizes and none are good or beneficial. It's something you could almost get away with in your late teens because at that age, you are experimenting with the power you have over people who are attracted to you. But, by the time you get into your twenties, it comes across as immature.

Games can include waiting to reply to messages, making people wait by turning up late to a date, making people jump through hoops, and I am sure you have experienced more. Some believe that these types of games add to the mystery and intrigue in a relationship, but it is more likely that the other person will get bored and look elsewhere. It is also a rather passive-aggressive habit that becomes hard to break.

JUMPING TO CONCLUSIONS

Even when we think we don't, we may make judgements about people before giving them a fair chance. This isn't just relating to looks. I have a thing about age and height. Any date that looked too young and I would immediately assume they were not mature enough. My husband is actually the same height as me; if I had assumed that he wasn't the one based on his height, I would probably still be dating today.

We do the same with behaviour. A man who talks about his mother too much could be called a mummy's boy and you come to the conclusion that she has far too much influence over him. It could be that his dad was abusive, and he is protective and proud of his mum. We don't know until the relationship has had time to develop and you learn more about him.

There is no such thing as a perfect person. There is, however, the perfect person for you. If you jump to conclusions early on, it is possible that the perfect person for you will be rejected on the basis of something that is either untrue or not significant enough to make a difference.

Your instincts are normally right and if your impression about someone doesn't change after a few dates, then at least you know you have given them a fair chance. Allow enough time to pass before you reach your conclusions.

FEELING THE NEED TO FIX SOMEONE

I think it's necessary to date one bad boy, just so you can add it to your list of experiences, and probably learn that this isn't the way you want to go. For some reason, we think that we are going to be the one that can change them and make them into a good man. The first problem here is that if you are looking for a good man, you should be dating good men, not bad boys. Bad boys are for fun and you won't change them, as they are happy the way they are.

It is possible to have an obsession with being a fixer-upper. We see something and feel the need to make it better. Our partner becomes our project. It might be the clothes they wear, their hairstyle, and then there are the domestic chores—this is a great one.

As much as we want to believe in equality, we aren't quite there yet and while there are men who will do their share, it's rare. How many fights have you had with your partner about this? You both work full-time; however, the home is still mainly your responsibility. So, we work on trying to change this.

I recognised my own mistake once. My husband finally hung the washing out (I think it had taken three years) but instead of praising him, I complained that the T-shirts and trousers were upside down and that the socks weren't matched. Why did I feel the need to change him? Couldn't he just hang the washing out as he wanted to?

Like we have mentioned, nobody is going to be perfect, but we have to accept the flaws that the other person has, instead of trying to fix them. Suppose you can't be with a person for their good and their bad. In that case, they aren't the right person for you, and you should consider ending the relationship before someone gets seriously hurt.

Remember there is a difference between showing someone new things and trying to fix them. Going to new places, trying new food, or recommending a new book is a way for both of you to learn new things together and to spark new conversations. It's when you start forcing things on your partner that means you want them to change. It works both ways, like the date that insisted on ordering a bottle of red wine because he knew I would like it if I tried it. Maybe I would, but I am big enough and brave enough to make that decision myself.

NOT TRUSTING A PERSON

Trust is incredibly difficult for anyone and if you have been cheated on, more so. The pain was so excruciating that you cannot risk going through it again and so you put up a protective barrier around you and will not let anyone in.

The logical side of us knows that not all men cheat, but our heart often wins this battle. As hard as this is, it's not fair to assume that this partner is going to hurt you. You must start each relationship with a fresh perspective and give the person a fair chance.

The first thing you need to do is learn to trust yourself. It may be that you chose the wrong man in the past, but it was a mistake and you are normally very good at making the right decisions. Learn to have faith in yourself and that you have made the right choice on this date.

If you are dating again, it should mean that you have had time to work through your emotions and you have left the awful experience in the past. If you are unable to trust someone, you might need to work on resolving your issues before dating. Trust can't be forced or unnatural, you can't tell your partner that you trust them but then question their every move.

THE GREAT FEMINISM DEBATE

Can you be a feminine feminist? Sometimes I feel like we are struggling to find the right balance and failing miserably. It hurt me when I heard that my friend went on a march for women's rights and then had to go home to get the dinner ready. We know what we want but not how to get it, or some people just don't know what they want.

It's not often I say this, but with regards to this subject, I feel sorry for men. How on Earth do they know whether or not they should hold the door open for a woman? Damned if they do, damned if they don't. A woman might want to be kissed, but does he have to ask permission or does he risk being accused of sexual assault? The move towards equality has brought about many great things; nevertheless, it has also made dating rather complex.

Men like an element of femininity. While they respect a high achiever, they don't want to feel like an employee in the relationship. We need to be careful that while defending our rights as females, we don't become too masculine and lose our sensuality.

Being feminine doesn't mean you need to put on a skirt, a pair of heels and a bit of makeup. Feminine qualities are hard to define. It is more important that we display feminine characteristics, like being kind and caring. It's a tough one, but the best thing is to be true to yourself.

RUSHING THROUGH THE DATING EXPERIENCE

Because dating is hard and we tend to label each date as a success, or more often a failure, we can come to see it as a chore. It's like that mountain of ironing: as soon as you get it over with, you can read your book or go out. If we can hurry through dating, we can move onto better things, like a loving relationship.

But is it really worth rushing through it to get it wrong and have to start over again or to end up in a meaningless relationship with no love? Imagine you are making a cake. You need to get the sponge right before you can think about decorating it. A beautiful cake has to taste amazing too. Dating is your sponge; take time in getting the right, and use quality ingredients so that the end result is perfect. You have your entire life to be with this one person. If it is love you are looking for, your dating days are short, so make the most of them while you can.

Consider why you feel the need to speed things up and miss out on the fun and excitement of dating. Sometimes we create a timeline that we need to stick too. All of your friends are sticking to that timeline, but you are behind. Really, you aren't behind at all, because everyone is so different. I had a friend who, at thirty-eight, was royally dumped and her long-term relationship came to an abrupt ending. A year later she was pregnant with her Mr Right. Another friend is my age and has three children with her high-school sweetheart. There is no right or wrong when it comes to how long you date, when you choose to move in with someone or get married, or even whether or not you get married. Enjoy what each stage has to offer.

IT HAS TO BE MENTIONED...

Without wanting to sound old, put the phone away. It is just so rude. If your date gets theirs out, it's no excuse to get yours out: it's their lack of manners, not yours. It shouldn't even be on the table. If you want to show photos then find the right moment to do it, after dinner, for example. The problem is that so much of our life is online, it seems unthinkable to survive an entire dinner without your phone. Trust me, your conversations will be much more engaging, and you will learn more about each other without the constant pings!

These are called common mistakes for a reason. We are smart women, and we do not make these mistakes because we aren't intelligent or because we look for ways to mess up dating. At the time, each date and relationship made sense. Hindsight is a wonderful thing.

During my dating decade (almost two), I experienced a rollercoaster of emotions, from sheer joy to complete deflation. I also wanted to just get it over with, as well as making probably all of the mistakes I have mentioned at one point or another. Life would have been easier if I had known all that I do now, but on the same hand, I appreciate all the experiences I had that led me to where I am today.

Don't kick yourself for the mistakes that have been made. Whether you are twenty-five or fifty-five, it is not too late to begin enjoying the modern dating world. Being aware of the mistakes now means you can prevent them. That's not to say that your dates won't make mistakes, and you should acknowledge that you can't control everything. As long as you are having fun, you won't feel like your time is being wasted.

These mistakes don't mean that you should try to change who you are. If you like jeans and a nice top instead of a dress, don't feel you need to put on a dress in order to be more feminine. It will only make you feel uncomfortable. If you don't feel like you can talk about your expectations straight away, wait until you are more confident, so you know you can express yourself in the right way, as long as you don't feel like you are compromising on important things. It's about doing what feels right at the time.

So, now that you know what not to do, it's time to get into the swing of dating. Where to start in today's world? It is still possible to meet someone at a party or a bar, strike up a conversation and start dating. Don't rule this out, even though there are now alternatives. Let your friends set you up on blind dates. It would be a shame if the traditional way of finding dates were to be completely forgotten by future generations. On the other hand, convenience in a very busy world does encourage us to turn to the world of online dating.

3

THE ABCS OF ONLINE DATING

I was dead set against the idea of online dating. I still liked the idea of going out and meeting people face to face, and I was worried about the lies people tell online. After a very hard break up, I found myself living in a village of about 1,400 people—my chances were getting slimmer by the minute.

After a particularly tipsy night with two friends, and yes, I was still feeling sorry for myself, one friend had taken my phone and was tapping away, but I didn't have the energy to stop her.

The next morning, along with a nasty headache, I woke up to an online dating profile. Obviously, I was furious at first, but before I had a chance to phone my friend up and give her grief, I noticed that I had a few likes. This might not seem like much but for someone who was at rock bottom, I felt a hint of a flutter.

Then I had a few messages. People actually liked me and wanted to hear more. I checked the photo to make sure they weren't confused—and it really was me. After six years in a relationship, I got to flirt again without any fear of face-to-face rejection. To cut a few months short, I found my husband through an online dating site, in the same village where I lived. It would seem that I am not alone. In America, approximately one-third of married couples met online. In the UK, it was around 23% in 2015. Before you jump to create your profile, let's cover the bad before the good.

The first thing that you must always keep in mind is your safety. This applies to creating your profile and actually meeting dates. In no circumstance should you include personal details on your profile, including your date of birth, your address, your phone number, or your email address. This information can be used against you by cyber criminals trying to commit fraud. On a similar note, be careful with your financial details when it comes to paid sites. It is safer to use a credit rather than a debit card, as you are more likely to have protection against fraud; check with your bank before using any card for payment.

In terms of the first date, it should always be in a public place, but we will discuss this a little more when we talk about arranging a date with someone you met online. Let's look at the exciting steps of creating your online dating profile!

There are so many online dating sites now that it is worth thinking about choosing one that meets your needs. There are dating sites for those looking for a certain religion, dates with other women, casual relationships, and many of the paid sites are normally used for those who are looking for a more serious commitment. If you are new to online dating, the most popular sites and apps are a great place to start and have millions of users.

HOW TO CREATE YOUR ONLINE DATING PROFILE

The profile pic

It's the first thing that people see, and it is what is going to make them want to discover more about you (because although we hate to admit it, looks do matter). Needless to say, due to the recent increase in popularity, there are even studies on the success of profile photos. These studies show that:

- The right number of photos to upload is four to ten
- People wearing red are seen as more attractive
- Photos of the left side of the face perform better
- Photos with landscapes in the background also perform better

The rest is mostly common sense. Make sure there isn't anything obvious in the photo that will allow others to learn about your identity, like standing outside your workplace. It is also best if you are alone in your photos, just to save confusion.

Have a look at some profile pics of women and decide what image you get of these people. Sexy is good but too sexy and you are likely to attract people who are only looking for sex, which is fine if that is what you want.

Then there is our dear friend, Photoshop. As tempted as you are to edit your photo, is it really worth it? Let's say you have made a few positive changes to your profile picture and you go on a date, the lighting is right so they might not notice the extent of your editing. But ladies, what if it is a really good date and you wake up next to them in the morning? At some point, they are going to see your IT skills.

Now, I know the photo of you on holiday two years ago is a lovely photo of you and you look stunning, but it's two years old and photos must be recent. How would you feel if your online Brad Pitt from *'Meet Joe Black'* turned out to be real Brad Pitt from *'The Curious Case of Benjamin Button'*? If you haven't seen either film, do a quick internet search and you will see my point. As with your photoshopping skills, at some point, the other person is going to see the up-to-date version of you.

Oh, and one last photo tip... don't take a selfie in the bathroom: it's really not necessary when there are so many other places.

I have my mum's voice in my head: "just one nice, up-to-date photo of you smiling" is what you need for a profile pic.

Choosing the right username

Again, think safety first and don't include any information that links to you personally. It's amazing how much psychology plays a role in the impact of your username. Men are more attracted to usernames that include references to your physical appearance whereas women like usernames that link to intelligence or culture. If your username starts with a letter from the first half of the alphabet, you will have more edge on those from the second half of the alphabet.

Here are some examples of how much a username can give away about a person:

- BustyBlonde- you consider your boobs to be one of your most important features
- 6amSunriseSmile- you are more of an active, morning person with a hint of romance
- DanceTheShotsAway- implies you like to party
- RomComCentral- anyone who isn't interested in romantic comedies might skip past you
- LoveMyLab- it is important that the person you meet loves dogs

We could go on, but you get the idea. Notice the correct use of capitalisation. Here is why this is important:

- Imurdreamguy2000- I think he wants to murder me.
- ImYourDreamGuy2000- ahh, that makes sense.

Think about what you are looking for and put a fun twist on it for your username.

Writing your message

Writing a description of yourself is often harder than it sounds. You don't want to come across as too modest or too conceited. You want the person to have an accurate idea of who you are, but then you can't write a full-on essay, but then people tell you to be funny and all of a sudden, a five-minute job becomes a complete self-assessment test. This is one reason why it is worth getting a little help from a friend.

The first place to start is by reading through some of the other online profiles and what they have to say. I don't want to sound catty but there are some cringe-worthy expressions ("I will rock your world") that will quickly help you know what you don't want to say. Here are some of my top examples:

- "Your mum will love me"- hopefully, you are looking for a man who can make this decision without his mum's influence.
- "I can make you happy"- how do you know what will make this stranger happy?
- "I'm fun-loving, easy-going, and adventurous"- you and half of the women online
- "I love romantic nights in and fun nights out"- if this were your CV, you have just used the

equivalent of "I work well on my own and in a team."

One of the problems with writing the message is that we often play it safe and use phrases that are commonly used, like some of those above. None of this will tell the person about who we really are.

When you use the words 'fun' or 'active', it can mean one thing to you and another to someone else. We need to be more specific about these adjectives. Hiking in the mountains and having a full social life are both examples of being active. Personally, I don't like the phrase "I am different from other women". In the first place, if lots of women use the same expression, it doesn't make us different. You need to explain why you are different. Do you have an extra toe or can you down a pint faster than any man? I have tried and found it very difficult to explain how I am different from other women in a short online-dating profile. When there are so many things you could say, it's best to steer clear of the word 'different'.

Another thing that you don't want to mention is your unsuccessful love life, your failed relationship, or the divorce you are going through. There is absolutely nothing wrong with looking for a date while you are in the midst of a divorce, but talking about it goes against dating etiquette. It's a cliché, but I have been on a date where the guy talked about his ex for the whole three hours! You do the right thing and start off being understanding and appreciate his sensitive side, but after the first hour you know he isn't ready to move on.

The theory is the same with your profile message. We have seen profiles with two paragraphs about why a person has given up on love and doesn't want to be hurt anymore and the last sentence is "...but I'm a fun person." Mixed signals there! You can't assume that every date is going to be the same as a past relationship. Focus your message on you and your positive side.

One mistake people often make is announcing their intelligence and then forgetting to spell check. This reminds me of a hilarious Ecard I once saw:

"The fact that you failed to spell check your online dating profile gives me serious doubts about your attention to detail in bed."

Be careful not to add too many ellipses (...) and LOLs. The overuse of the ellipsis makes it difficult to follow what a person is saying. The same can be said with the overuse of any punctuation mark or acronym. You don't need numerous LOLs to show someone that you are in touch with the latest lingo. English can be a crazy language and it's normal to make mistakes, but watch out for the biggies like 'your' and 'you're'.

Finally, and this is more of a personal one for me because not everyone will agree, take care when using the word 'should'. Should is usually used for advice, but it can also be used for small obligations. Do you really want your potential date to feel like they are being told what to do at such an early stage? This is what I mean:

"You should love pets as much as I do". The reader may think "Should I? And what if I don't?". Consider rephrasing to something like "I'm looking for someone who loves pets as much as I do". Like I said, perhaps it's just me, but the word 'should' may come across as a little aggressive in an online dating profile.

Examples of Good Online Dating Profile Messages

'I love meeting new people and trying new activities such as outdoor sports and visiting different places. I would love to meet someone who wants to travel more and explore new cultures.'

'If I had to choose one type of music, I would say dance, although I'm probably happier dancing around my house than going to clubs. I wouldn't say no to going to any type of concert, except for heavy rock. Favourite films—The Godfather trilogy.'

'If something serious were to develop that would be great, but at the moment, I am looking for someone who is respectful and has direction in their own life. More than anything, I want to spend time with someone who makes me laugh.'

You can get a sense that this profile is not of someone in their late teens/early twenties. For a "fresher" approach, you can add in quotes of what other people say about you, for example:

'Best friend says: "Her craziness is contagious", ex says "like a fine wine, gets better with age."'

What also works is the more/less description—sweet < savoury, mountains > beach. This is a great way to keep things simple and clearly show what you are all about.

AND WHEN THE MESSAGES START COMING IN?

It's like all of your birthdays and Christmases in one. When those messages come in you will get the biggest rush of positive emotions from excitement to shock. You will feel sexy, desired, hopefully, even nervous. You'll feel sixteen again and it's no exaggeration. For the first time in perhaps a long time, you will remember what it is like to feel confident about yourself. It's the beginning of a new phase and you might find yourself motivated to try different things.

Don't forget that there is no need to play a passive role in online dating. Men do like it when women make the first move and after all, it's only a message. If you don't feel like you are getting the right attention, it's now time to start checking out some profiles. If you see a profile that you like, send a short message to introduce yourself. It's a game of Law of Averages: the more people you speak to, the more opportunities you have to date people who you will be attracted to and with whom you will have things in common.

When replying to messages, you need to remember to keep it short, at least for the first few messages. The ideal length is around two hundred words. If you start going over this, you reduce the chances of getting a reply. These messages allow you to show off your personality and to say those things that you really wanted to mention in your profile but didn't have the space. Topics should be general and light; again, there probably isn't any need to mention the ex just yet.

While the adrenaline rush is amazing, don't be so excited that you forget to read their message completely. Trust me, you don't want to read the first few lines, but skip the part that says he has just been released on bail and living with his mum and her forty cats. Look for things you have in common and ask questions about those and about other things that interest you about their profile. Try to keep a balance between the "I" statements and the "you" statements.

If there is anything that doesn't sit right with you or if your instincts are ringing alarm bells, don't feel obliged to meet them. Never meet people who aren't going to respect your boundaries. It's highly unlikely that this person is going to be a good match for you in the future. There is no need to agree to meet someone because you fear there won't be other chances. There will!

We have already mentioned mind games, like making people wait for a response. It's not a good way to start a new relationship and when it comes to online dating, there are so many fish in the sea, it simply won't work. Respond to messages as soon as you can. If you are rushed off your feet, send a quick message saying you will answer properly when you get a chance.

At the same time, don't feel like you have to rush into giving them your phone number, or arranging to meet them. Sometimes you can start talking to someone and within a few days you have a good sense of who they are, or it may take a couple of weeks. Enjoy each stage for what it is without feeling pressured into moving forward. You will know when the time is right to meet.

Now here is the real fun part and something that I got wrong the first time (ok, the first few times). We aren't women living in the nineteenth century, where one man knocks on our door and after one romantic walk in the park we are betrothed. The twenty-first-century woman keeps her options open and is proud to do so.

WHAT IS THIS GHOSTING THING ALL ABOUT?

About five years ago, those in the dating world, and more so the online dating scene, were introduced to ghosting. If you have ever been messaging someone, things seem to be going well and then you never hear from them again, you have been ghosted!

It's quite horrible really and it's normal if you feel a little hurt. The truth is, ghosting is the downside to being able to enjoy online anonymity. Because you are unlikely to bump into the person in your local supermarket or when you are out with friends, it is easier to cut off all communication without feeling guilty or experiencing repercussions.

As hard as it sounds, if you are ghosted, try not to take it personally. If it has its own term, it's because it happens all the time and it is something we need to accept. Don't let it knock your confidence. Ghosting says more about the other person than it does you. And if it does happen to you, remember how painful it is so that you are discouraged from doing it to someone else.

MEETING DATES YOU HAVE MET ONLINE

Our aim at this point is to meet nine people face to face. I'm going to pretend I didn't hear the twenty-first-century shout "nine?" in shock! Though you might feel that you are incapable of choosing between two options, our brains can handle between five and nine. Whether you call it a date or just a few drinks, as long as you are honest with yourself, you can meet more than one person. It's also important that you are honest with them. If you are meeting other people, it is better to let them know rather than to start a relationship on a lie. On a practical note, don't get their names wrong. I had a friend who was meeting three guys whose names all began with J and I'm not sure how she pulled that off.

The first meeting should be limited to about one hour. Dinner is a great idea, but it leaves you with few options to leave if things aren't working out. Drinks or coffee are perfect for two reasons: there is no pressure to call it a date and you have more control over the amount of time you spend with them. Also, you are in a public place, which means you will be safer than meeting them alone. A romantic dinner at his house sounds like every girl's dream, but please, not the first time you meet someone. I know I sound like your mum, but while talking about safety, always tell someone where you are going and who you are going with.

During these first few meetings, there will be things you like and things you may not like. It's too easy for us to make a decision based on something that is trivial, or to ignore something that is significant for us. So, they are wearing jeans and trainers and that makes the hairs on the back of your neck stand up, but is this enough to not want to learn more? If you are religious and your date is cursing God left, right and centre, is this something that you will be able to tolerate?

I went on a first date after meeting someone online and I must admit, I made the rookie mistake of agreeing to a second date when I shouldn't have. He was so funny, which to me was something that was very important. But he kept burping! Obviously, I laugh about this now. At the time, it was something that I couldn't see myself getting past, especially when people around us started looking... at me! I put it down to nerves and thought the next date would be different. Surprise, surprise, it wasn't.

Speaking of nerves, not every date is full of chemistry and lust. There are so many other things going on, like nerves, tension, or worry. It is hard to relax and be yourself on the first date, so give them at least three dates to see if an attraction develops. Don't fall into the trap of "he/she isn't my type". I hate to be blunt, but your type hasn't been working all that well, so this is the perfect time to explore other types that you might have misjudged previously.

When you are looking through profiles online, you aren't or at least shouldn't be looking for 'The One'. You are putting too much pressure on something that should be fun and enjoyable. Remember how you felt when you first started getting messages. Do you really want to give that up straight away? Keep messaging people, keep meeting people, and keep learning more about yourself. This is how you will meet someone who is perfectly suited to you. Get to know your date before you choose your wedding dress—yes, been there and done that, as I'm sure you have too.

There has been a lot of dos and don'ts in this chapter, so let's have a quick recap on how to meet people online successfully.

Dos and Don'ts for Your Profile:

- Do be honest
- Do upload a recent photo of yourself
- Do include photos that show your interests
- Do create a fun username that reflects who you are
- Do mention specifics about your likes and dislikes
- Do reply to messages as soon as you can
- Don't give out any personal details
- Don't photoshop your images
- Don't use generic expressions that everyone uses
- Don't waffle
- Don't wait for people to message you
- Don't take it personally if you don't hear back from someone

Do's and Don'ts for Meeting Dates

- Do take your time when arranging to meet someone
- Do meet as many people as you want
- Do make sure that you meet in a public place
- Do tell someone else where you are going and who you are going with

- Do stick to your boundaries
- Don't plan an activity that forces you to stay in an uncomfortable situation
- Don't feel pressured into doing anything you don't want to do
- Don't judge people on the first date
- Don't expect chemistry when you are both likely to be nervous
- Don't arrange a second date if there are characteristics that you know you can't tolerate

Above all, remember to have fun. Even if, after a few dates, you don't feel like it is going how you had hoped, you have to appreciate the experiences you have had. It doesn't mean that you have failed. If you start to meet dates with the attitude that it isn't going to work, they will pick up on this. Each date should feel fresh and exciting with plenty of butterflies.

Let's say that up until now, you have had a few successful 'meetings' and it is time to arrange a proper first date. You might have begun to feel less nervous but don't be surprised if it all starts to come flooding back when you make it an official date. We are going to use this nervous energy to enjoy ourselves.

4

A RECIPE FOR A MAGICAL FIRST DATE

We have so many expectations on a first date that it's hard for things to turn out as perfectly as we had hoped. Your date might be just how you hoped they looked and when they smile, the twinkle in the eyes, the perfect smile. Then the conversation is easy and comfortable, the lights dim at just the right time and then your favourite song begins to play. It is possible, but these expectations are often a little too high.

I think I was about sixteen when I had my first date. We had seen each other around, had a few conversations, exchanged numbers and I felt so grown up when he invited me to his house for dinner. He was twenty-three, so I hadn't expected dinner to be at his parent's house. Nor had I expected his sweet mum to cook and serve the dinner. It wasn't quite the magic I had envisioned.

While we have heard of plenty worse (the funeral director who picked up his date in a hearse that was occupied, the man who kept "running to the bathroom", only for the waiter to tell the woman he was on another date on the other side of the restaurant, etc.), first dates carry a lot of weight. They can exceed expectations, not quite meet them, or they can be an absolute disaster. One of the biggest problems with first dates is the expectations we have. There are things we can do to ensure that our first date goes as well as it can, and despite sounding a bit Disneyfied, they can be magical, but it's important that we leave our expectations in the past.

FIRST DATE PREPARATION

As you are getting ready for a first date, there will already be a number of things running through your mind. It's insulting to think that the only thing we worry about is what to wear. You will still be nervous, concerned about whether you are making the right decision, or if you are meeting in the right place. The reason the scene where Bridget Jones is getting ready, choosing between the sexy pants and the sucky-in pants, is so funny is because it is so true. What are you going to talk about? What if you dribble sauce all down your top? And yes, what are you going to wear?

Let's get the whole outfit out of the way. It shouldn't matter, but it does and maybe not for the reason you are thinking. What you wear will affect your confidence, possibly a lot. You want to look smart, sexy, comfortable, and elegant. I certainly don't have one outfit that says all of that and makes me look slim at the same time. Rule number one: dress for comfort. Short dresses are lovely, but if you spend all night pulling it down to cover your bum you will feel paranoid and look twitchy. A little bit of boob is good, but regardless of your age or size, you don't want to run the risk of falling out of your top or having to fish a bit of food out of your cleavage. Sexy has once again backfired. My three outfit-picking tips that will suit most types of first dates are:

A nice pair of jeans or the good old black trousers —these are some of the most comfortable clothes that can be dressed up or down for any situation

A top that shows a bit of skin and a bit of cleavage (don't laugh but I say 2-3 fingers)—add some colour or sparkle to your outfit

Shoes or boots with a small heel—heels make you feel tall and confident, but too high and I just fall over.

This outfit makes me feel comfortable and sexy but it's not everyone's cup of tea. Choose clothes and accessories that make you feel good about yourself and not what you think you should wear. If you aren't used to wearing makeup, don't feel you need to just because it's a date.

Another rookie mistake I made was to have a glass of wine while I was getting ready one night. "It will calm my nerves", I convinced myself. One became two, plus another one when we arrived at the restaurant and I was halfway to drunk before the starter arrived.

Calm your nerves by thinking positively about yourself. Focus on your good qualities, your skills and your talents. If need be, do some yoga or have a workout before getting ready to calm your inner self.

CHOOSING THE RIGHT LOCATION

Again, the pressure is immense. There are so many ways things can go wrong. I had a date who insisted we go to a seafood restaurant once. I hate seafood, I hate fish. But he knew best and I ate bread. Dinner for your first date is a sound choice. It provides a good atmosphere to get to know each other better without too much noise, but it should be a restaurant that serves food that you both like.

It should also be a neutral restaurant. Your date might feel uncomfortable if you know all of the staff by their first name and keep bumping into people you know. If the other person has chosen the location, do a little research on it first.

When it comes to the meal itself, order what you want. Listen to recommendations from your date and offer your opinions, but you should be able to eat what you feel like eating. My date and I both ordered a salad one night and smiled as we munched through our rabbit food. The date went well so we decided to go out to a bar afterwards. Embarrassingly, after two hours we both admitted to being starving and went to get a burger and chips.

And the bill? Never assume that they are going to pay. Ladies, we can't have it both ways. We can't want to date like modern women, but then expect to have our meals paid for like the good old days. The least you should do is the 'cheque dance'—both hands go on the bill and you slide it back and forward saying "I'll get this" and "No, let me". Suggest splitting the bill and if they insist, then so be it. But insist that it's your turn next time, and don't conveniently forget.

Dinner is comfortable and comfortable is good, but it's not your only option. One of my best first dates was skating in a park. I had absolutely no idea what I was doing, but it was the perfect excuse to hold hands and any other part of each other as he tried to keep me upright. The following list has a few suggestions if you are looking for some different first date ideas:

- Bowling
- Picnic in the park
- Go to a museum
- Sign up for a cooking class
- Visit somewhere new in your city
- Play mini-golf
- Go for a walk, see the sunset or the sunrise

First dates don't have to be complicated or expensive. You must have the opportunity to talk to each other, so things like the cinema where you will sit in silence for at least two hours might not be best. Those days or weeks that you spend messaging with each other should have given you some inspiration for a fun first date.

THE ESSENTIALS OF FIRST DATE CONVERSATION

It is so awkward when everything is going well and then all of a sudden, the conversation just dies, or worse, you say something that the other person takes offence to. First date conversations should be about getting to know each other better. It's the perfect time to learn more about each other's interests and hobbies, places that you have travelled to and where you still want to go. This is the time when you can find out about family and careers. You can talk about the music and films that you both like, and don't worry if they aren't all the same. My husband hates Pink and I hate flamenco, but we work around this.

There are certain topics that should be avoided at this early stage. From as young as I can remember, my grandparents had the rule of no religion or politics at the dinner table. It's something that has stuck with me and is a good rule for first dates. The problem with such topics is that we normally have very strong opinions about them, and this can lead to conflict. If not conflict, then it will surely lead to some awkward moments. The same can be said about financial situations and plans for the future. How much you earn has little to do with whether or not you will be well-suited to each other. If a man asked you how many children you wanted, you would probably be somewhat taken back; it's the same the other way around. It's not that these conversations should never be discussed, but there is plenty to talk about before hitting the hardcore topics.

To make your first date conversations flow, I have a few conversation starters that have always worked well. They not only give you the chance to learn more about each other but also start a ton of other conversations.

1. The Great Dinner Party Question

If you could choose any ten people, dead or alive to invite for dinner, who would you invite and why? This question provides insight into who they respect and admire. Don't freak out if he says Julia Roberts, Brittney Spears or Cleopatra. Each to their own and I'm sure you would choose at least one hot man or woman! The best answer I ever had was "Jesus Christ, so that he could turn all the water into wine!" You can follow up with the food you would serve and the after-dinner entertainment.

2. Would You Rather...?

Would you rather be a bird or a dolphin?

Would you rather eat insects or never eat meat again?

Would you rather live without music or TV?

Would you rather have the same haircut or the same phone for the rest of your life?

. . .

The list is endless, and you might find they will join in with a few ideas of their own.

3. If...?

If money was no object, what would you do?

If you could go anywhere in the world, where would you go?

If you could start a new hobby, what would it be?

If you could have any job, what would you do?

Similarly to 'Would you Rather', you can choose any type of question from the silly to the important, depending on what you feel is appropriate.

Bear in mind that these types of conversation starters are just that. They are ways to start new conversations, not to make the other person feel like they are being interviewed. It is essential that you make just as much effort to listen to their answers as you do to ask the questions.

Only ask questions that you would be comfortable answering. Somebody once asked me if I would rather kill ten family members or a thousand strangers. The question revolted me and though I probably should have politely explained that I wasn't comfortable answering that type of question, I left immediately.

We have boundaries for a reason. They help us with our communication. They allow others to understand more about our values and beliefs, and they encourage people to respect what matters to us. If you aren't comfortable answering a question, politely explain this. Let the person know from day one that some boundaries won't be crossed. You can be assertive without being rude or aggressive and it will allow you to have a deeper, more meaningful relationship in the future.

Like our first meetings, it is still not the right time to bring up the ex in conversations. Your mind might start to wonder to the mistakes that were made and to comparing your date to your ex. For now, we are still looking at fresh starts and not those nasty assumptions that you might be tempted to make.

What to do about jokes? It's a tricky one. I am the first one to admit to a bizarre sense of humour and I find some jokes about women funny when I shouldn't, but this is because I am the woman in the joke, if that makes sense. I have grown to be able to laugh at my faults rather than take offence. However, unless the joke is clean and politically correct, I would tread very carefully. At this point, you are still not fully aware of the other person's sense of humour and they might not find the same joke funny.

TO FLIRT OR NOT TO FLIRT?

The answer is much easier in theory than in practice! If you feel like there is a genuine connection and the first signs of attraction are flourishing, it is natural to want to flirt. If you don't feel this way, then don't do it. It doesn't mean that you give up on a second or third date. But it is unfair to start flirting and leading your date into thinking you have feelings when you don't.

Flirting is a subtle way of telling someone that you are interested. The keyword is subtle. When a woman starts giggling at everything their date says, she is going overboard. Too much winking and you go from flirting to looking like you have something in your eye. I remember trying to go for a flirty hair flick, only to have most of it end up in my mouth.

Successful flirting comes down to three key ingredients —humour, wit, and smart conversations. Imagine flirting as being like your car engine that won't start. You need to give it just the right amount of gas; too much and you are going to flood the engine.

Every now and then, it is worth brushing up on your flirting skills, especially if you have just come out of a long-term relationship. If you have had a knock to your confidence, you might feel like you have completely forgotten how to flirt. Don't panic, you're smart and you will take to flirting in today's dating scene like a duck to water.

Practice your flirting online- That moment when you send your first kiss emoji and wonder if you have gone too far, just to get one back a few minutes later. You can even just send a nice text: "My day gets better when I hear from you". Flirting online is a good way to dip your toe in the water and get a feel for flirting again.

Be yourself- Your date is interested in you because of the profile you created... about yourself. There is no need for you to feel like you have to be anyone except for yourself.

Eye contact- This is a great place to start, because you do this all the time when you are communicating with friends. The only difference is that you want to hold the eye contact for just a couple of seconds longer. Too long and they will feel uncomfortable. For a little more intimacy, you can allow your gaze to fall over their lips. Again, just for a few seconds. You don't want them thinking they have food all around their mouth.

Mirror each other's energy- it might be that you laugh when they laugh, or it could be a gentle brush of the hand. It is important that it is mutual and natural. Grabbing a hand to hold might be crossing a boundary, so you need to follow each other's lead and make sure you are both comfortable, particularly with physical contact.

Choose your words wisely- You can flirt with your words. Compliments are a lovely way to show your interest. Kind words and a bright smile are enough to melt me! And the type of compliment also makes a big difference. "That is such a smart way to look at things", with the right eye contact and a smile and you have nailed it! Don't forget to compliment men on their outfit; they too may have spent a while deciding what to wear. Compliments about someone's physique may come off too strong, if you are looking for something more than physical.

Show that you are listening- someone who listens, I mean really listens, is sexy. It shows that they are not only interested in themselves. Reflect the things they have said in your answers "So, you want to change your job. What would you like to do?" It doesn't sound sexy, but it is.

Genuinely enjoy yourself- when you have picked the right outfit and ordered the meal you really wanted to, you will have fun. Having fun on your date will send off positive vibes, help you both to relax, so flirting becomes easier.

JUST HOW FAR DO YOU GO ON A FIRST DATE?

It wouldn't be a very good dating book if we didn't answer the difficult questions. Do you have sex on the first date or not? For years, we have lived behind the idea that if we jump into bed with a man on the first date, they will assume we are "easy" and we will never find real love. And who on Earth came up with this, or the rule of waiting until the third date? Talk about pressure! As two consenting adults in the throes of passion, are you going to stop and say "sorry, we have reached our first date quota"?

Times have changed a great deal and so has our view of sex on the first date. Because of online dating, it has become easier to talk about sex, even to talk about what turns us on, before we meet for the first date. This has helped to take the pressure off sex. Your online flirting may have been so amazing that you struggle to get through dinner without wanting to get your hands on each other.

The statistics from a recent study show just how much our opinions on the matter have changed. Over a third of men fell in love with their partner who they had sex with on the first date. 56% of women had sex with their partner on the first date. So, to assume that you won't be able to form a serious commitment is wrong.

Waiting can intensify the passion, and this is awesome —if this is what you want. If you have just made it around the mini-golf course and the moment is now, that is awesome. Nobody can judge you for doing what you feel is right. Sex, like dating, is yours to own and you should go as fast or slow as you feel comfortable.

On this subject, I have to take just a second to think about your safety. You need to be able to trust your instincts. If there is the slightest bit of doubt, you say no. If there is pressure from your date to have sex and you don't want to, you say no. If a man refuses to use protection, you say no. These are my absolute musts for safe sex and don't let your raging hormones let you fall for the "just this once will be ok".

You also need to be careful about how much you drink. Drunk first date sex is hilarious and youthful, but it can lead to regrets if it is the alcohol that is making decisions for you. It also opens the door to awkward moments.

My own little rule is that first date sex should always be in your own home. There is an extra element of security when you are in your own home.

Don't let other people's opinions affect your decision. As long as you are sensible and safe, take the bull by the horns, so to speak, and have fun.

YOUR GET OUT OF JAIL FREE CARD

Sometimes, the date just isn't going to go well, and this is nobody's fault. Think of it as trying to make a new dish and it was terrible. You followed the recipe to the letter, but it wasn't to your taste. You won't make it again.

You should have a Get Out of Jail Free card or in other words, an escape strategy. A while ago I was watching the TV show *First Dates* (call it an occupational hazard) and I was baffled by the number of terrible excuses I saw. Here were my favourites:

- I have a headache
- My aunt is in the hospital
- My best friend has just been dumped
- My dog is sick
- My boss has called me into work

I mean, seriously? Unless your date is incredibly stupid, they will see right through this. The fake phone call is still very common but sitting on the opposite side of the table watching your put on a far-from-Oscar-winning performance is really not necessary. Having a friend waiting to bail you out of a disastrous date is a good plan for when you feel uncomfortable and are concerned about how the other person will react when you try to cut things short. It is also a good security blanket to have.

On the same program, I watched a couple who were both attractive, smart, had a good career, but something wasn't going right. The woman received her fake emergency phone call and the man laughed and said that he couldn't believe she got to use her fake phone call first. There was something about that moment that completely changed the date and they ended up getting on really well.

This is probably the only case I have ever seen of the fake emergency call actually resulting in something positive. If things aren't going as you had hoped, be honest and don't insult the other person's intelligence. Don't tell them you will call them when you have no intention of doing so. It only gives them false hope and it's not something that you would like done to you.

This is another reason why it is important to ensure your first date is in a public place. If, for any reason, things turn ugly and you feel threatened or uncomfortable, there are people around you that you can turn to for help.

When planning your first date, be sure to let your date know that you have a limited amount of time. If things are going really well, you can extend this time. However, if things aren't going so well, it will be much easier for you to end the date, because they are already aware that the time is up.

Some people will tell you to do a runner. I would only do this if they are rude, arrogant, or you don't feel safe. If it's just that you don't feel like the date is going in the right direction, the politest and most respectful thing to do is to tell them that you are leaving.

When you tell someone that the date isn't going as planned, you should keep it short and simple while being assertive. My favourite sentence is: "I'm sorry to cut this short, but I don't think this is going the way we had hoped". There is no need to follow up with more, and avoid clichés like "It's not you, it's me". If they ask why, you can explain your feelings but without making it personal. Maybe you thought you would have more in common or you were looking for someone with similar goals to yours. Be honest and imagine how you would like to be treated if things were the other way around. Insulting someone may only encourage them to become angry.

If you have been out of the dating scene for a while, it all might sound overwhelming, especially when we start talking about an exit strategy for when you date loses the plot. Remember that this is very, very rare. More than anything, it's a 'better safe than sorry' type of thing, just in case! Don't let this put you off.

Even when I started getting better at dating, there were still a few cringeworthy moments that almost made me feel like I was taking steps back rather than forward. The best thing I could tell myself was that without the bad dates, what stories would I have to tell my children, or my nieces and nephews when they were navigating their way through these unknown territories? You have to look for the good in every situation!

We have said this before, but you need to take some time to get to know the person through messages and get a feel for what they are like. This, along with your common sense and intuition, should eliminate the risk of meeting anyone who is not quite with it. When you add a comfortable yet sexy outfit and the right amount of eye contact, you are ready for a magical date.

In the next chapter, we are going to start looking at turning those dates into something more intimate, both physically and emotionally. And yes, we will be exploring the sexual side of intimacy to ensure that the honeymoon period in the bedroom doesn't fizzle away.

5

COMMUNICATION AND BUILDING INTIMACY

The magical first date turned into a second and third magical date and you are floating on cloud nine. I also hope that if you aren't floating on cloud nine you have gone back to your inbox to line up more new people. But let's go back to things going well and you having a great feeling about a future between you and this special person.

At this stage, you still might feel that the romance is a bit of a rollercoaster, but not because there are ups and downs in terms of how well you are getting on. It's true that you may have discovered the odd thing that niggles you, but it's certainly not a deal-breaker. The ups and downs at this point are more to do with the speed in which things progress. You may question when and how to start revealing things about yourself. You might be wanting things to become more serious, but you fear pushing it in case you come across too strong. You might feel that you are now ready to become more physically intimate, but the analogy of riding a bike really isn't appropriate.

Taking things to the next level should also bring about a similar sort of feeling as those first few dates did. It should be exciting, although it is normal that you feel nervous. The last thing you want to do is to burst the happy bubble that you have just created. It doesn't have to be this way. You can maintain this level of euphoria as the relationship develops if you learn how to communicate properly at this stage.

We are going to break this down into three sections: communication, intimacy, and communication with regards to intimacy. As well as finding out how we can learn to improve our communication, we are going to discover how to set boundaries so that we express our feelings and desires with confidence.

BECOMING A BETTER COMMUNICATOR IN THE EARLY STAGES OF A RELATIONSHIP

Communication is a funny thing. It's crazy to think that we utter our first few words as toddlers, but we can be in our twenties, thirties, fifties, or even retired and still not know how to communicate well. A common misconception is that communication is about others being able to understand your message clearly. Obviously, this is a part of it, but just a small part. Communication can be verbal, non-verbal, written, and visual. It is said that communication should be approximately 40% talking and 60% listening. It can be something as straightforward as "I love you" or as complex as a look between each other that only you understand.

Humans spent so long learning how to be book-smart that we lost the importance of being emotionally smart. A genius can understand the neuroscience and chemical reactions in the brain that lead us to feel love, but they can still struggle to explain to a non-scientist what love is.

WHY IS COMMUNICATION COMPLICATED?

You have spent years getting to know your friends and appreciating how each of you communicates in different ways, even longer with certain family members. Even now, you may still struggle to get your point across or look at them blankly as they explain something to you. Communication is a skill that needs to be learnt and practised and quite frankly, I still take all the help I can get, because as times change, I don't think it is ever something that we will become perfect at. But that's ok.

Communication can be broken down into the message and the receiver. The message can be the same for ten different people, but every receiver has their own way of filtering information and individual explanatory styles. We will interpret a message depending on our filters and styles. It's like when you and your friend are singing different lyrics to the same song or when you see blue and she sees green.

By now, you have probably got to know your new romance a little better. Conversations about day-to-day life and the easy subjects flow well. Now is a good time to start testing the water and asking those more difficult questions or opening up more about yourself.

Try not to put too much pressure on these conversations; after all, they are still only things you are talking about. Asking someone if they could see themselves getting married isn't the same as asking them to get married. In fact, this is quite a good question to start or with, because you can giggle at the panic and remind them that you aren't proposing.

SETTING BOUNDARIES WITHIN A NEW RELATIONSHIP

This is also the right time to start creating and expressing your boundaries. Don't fall into the trap of thinking that your partner should be able to figure out what your wants and needs are. Boundaries can reduce communication confusion; however, they need to be expressed first.

When setting boundaries, you need to be self-aware in terms of your likes and dislikes and more specifically, what you are comfortable with and where the limit is. For example, you can be comfortable with trying new food, as long as it isn't forced upon you. You must be clear when you talk about boundaries. In the early days, it is still easy to misinterpret something which can later lead to an argument. Let's look at some good examples:

- "Can I just have ten minutes to finish what I am doing? Then I would love to hear about your day"- your partner will understand that you don't like to be interrupted but that you are still keen to listen to them.
- "I don't mind washing your clothes as long as they are always put in the washing basket"- you aren't a mum who has to go around picking up dirty clothes.

- "I will not be your nurse because you have a hangover"- it's important that the other person knows that their behaviour also has consequences.
- "I understand that you are angry, but I will not be shouted at"- draw a clear line about any type of verbal or physical abuse.

Needless to say, our boundaries are quite personal and vary a lot, but when I first looked at my boundaries, I realised that they weren't that easy to explain, which is why you need to take some time to know yours.

A common mistake I have seen is that people wait to mention a boundary until it has been crossed. I have absolutely no problem with my husband talking to other women. But when he sits there for five minutes and doesn't introduce me, I just feel this is rude. The first time I let it slide (mistake number one); the second time I made a little joke out of it because I didn't want to come across as jealous (mistake number two). As you can guess, the third time I exploded, and it turned into an argument where I was jealous! If my husband had known how I had felt, the problem would have been solved with a conversation.

COMMUNICATION ESSENTIALS

Let's take my situation from above and look at how I could have effectively communicated my feelings.

1. State the facts

Your partner may not be aware of any problem that has occurred. My husband finished his conversation, looked at me and asked if I wanted another drink, oblivious to my frustration. The fact is, I was ignored —"I didn't appreciate being left out of your conversation".

2. Explain how you feel

Hidden feelings are dangerous in a relationship. They are the accelerant in a fire and often lead to arguments. You need to learn to understand your own feelings first. My husband would assume that I was jealous, when in fact, I was embarrassed sitting there like I was nobody—"I felt embarrassed that you didn't introduce me to the other person, I felt like you were ashamed of me".

3. Tell the person what you need

If your partner doesn't hear you express what you need, how are they going to learn? Your message is incomplete—"I need to feel that when we are out together as a couple that you treat me like an equal partner, not as an accessory that you can leave at the table".

4. Make your request clear

Finally, your partner needs some direction, clear instructions that will prevent the same thing from happening again—"The next time you meet a friend, can you please introduce me to them?".

We aren't going to fall into the stereotypical opinions that it's only men that need help with communication. I love these four steps and at the beginning of my relationship, I started a conversation and we spoke about the best ways to communicate. This really helped us to set a solid foundation for when we needed to talk about the harder topics.

LISTENING MISTAKES

"We have two ears and one mouth so that we can listen twice as much as we speak"

— EPICTETUS, A GREEK PHILOSOPHER

Both men and women have moments when they don't listen. It's not really that we are bored, but the brain is so busy that we struggle to maintain our focus. The huge problem with this is that if we don't listen, we are unable to respond, and communication fails.

Common listening mistakes include:

- Daydreaming, imagining what you are going to cook for dinner, your to-do list for the next day, etc.
- Planning what to say next
- Making judgements about what the other person is saying
- Listening but expecting a certain outcome

If you are really honest with yourself, you can probably admit to making all of these mistakes at some point in a relationship, but also being on the receiving end of them. Bless my husband for allowing me to use him as an example, but he has a habit of talking forever. One short story goes on and on, even when he can see I am working. I have to wave my hands around frantically to speed him up, because if not, I know I will start thinking about the next chapter of my book or whether I should do some yoga.

To be a good listener, you need to begin with no bias and no presumptions of where the conversation is going. Listen for their emotions and react appropriately. If they are upset, hug them and show them that you care. Never interrupt with a solution because you haven't allowed them time to finish communicating their message. They may not even be looking for a solution, just someone to listen to them.

WHAT TO DO WHEN COMMUNICATION GOES DOWNHILL

There is not a couple in the world who haven't had an argument at some point, or maybe there is, but is this really healthy? Experts have coined the term "healthy arguments", where disagreements can actually turn out to be productive discussions. They allow the other person to see that you have strong emotions about something, your true feelings are expressed, and you can learn more about each other. Then there is the making up, which undoubtedly enables you to feel closer than you did before.

THE COMMUNICATION CLIMATE

When things turn difficult in a conversation, our natural flight-or-fight instinct kicks in. This is why some people shut down and retreat, while others blow like a volcano. In both of these situations, we end up in what is known as a destructive climate. This can cause the wrong type of language to be used or can lead to apathy (indifference). There are also behaviours that we aren't necessarily aware of, such as tensing up or crossing our arms.

When we fall into a defensive climate, we may feel that we are better than the other person or that we are more intelligent than them. It's that moment when you are convinced you are right and it's impossible to see any room for give and take. There might be a need for you to maintain control, so much so that you come up with hidden agendas.

When I say 'we', it is obviously not only limited to our side of the conversation. It is just as possible for your partner to become defensive. Both parties must be able to identify a defensive climate and learn how to take a step back. Walk away and calm down. When you are both in a better place, you can begin talking about the issue with a new perspective.

What we are looking to create is a supportive climate, as this is where both people can discuss their feelings and concerns without fear of repercussions and with mutual respect. A supportive climate is one that offers:

- an honest desire to take on board what the other person is saying
- the opportunity to find solutions together by discussing alternative options
- the eagerness to explore the situation in more depth
- an equal environment where both parties have a chance to be heard
- comfort so that both of you can speak in a direct manner
- affection, so you don't lose sight of what is really important

TEXTING YOUR WAY OUT OF A ROMANCE

With so much of our communication done online, it's easy to start or continue an argument by text. Personally, I wouldn't advise this. On the one hand, you can't shout and you have the opportunity to read and reread your message. On the other hand, you are missing the tone of voice and body language and this very easily leads to misinterpretations. Quite often, an argument that ends up on your smartphone can last a lot longer than it would if it had been face to face.

Relying on your phone for difficult conversations will mean you never learn how to talk to each other properly. Save texting for the fun stuff, an apology for arguing and a promise to make it up to them, kissing plus winking emoji.

On this note, when you do argue, please, put the phones down. There is nothing more aggravating than trying to have a serious conversation while the other person is tapping away on their mobile.

PUTTING A STOP TO PASSIVE AGGRESSIVE BEHAVIOUR STRAIGHT AWAY

Although I hate aggressive behaviour, I hate passive-aggressive behaviour more. There is malice to this, it's like your partner is going out of their way to make life more difficult but in a highly subtle way. It's a manipulation technique and it won't just disappear; it has to be stopped.

Somebody who is always late is being passive-aggressive. They are demonstrating that your time is not as important as theirs. The words "you're always right" is extremely passive-aggressive, as the person has decided to end the conversation without letting you explain your side. Then there are those people who purposely make half an effort to do a job, knowing that you will have to do it correctly.

Look out for signs of passive-aggressive behaviour early on. Resist the urge to nag, because it will have no positive impact. Get straight to the point and tell them that there is a problem that has to be resolved. Watch out for replies like "Why are you so mad?" They know why and it's part of the emotional game they play. Be determined when explaining the problem. They have probably been able to get away with it in other relationships, but as soon as they appreciate that you won't tolerate it, it shouldn't be a problem.

The main thing to remember when you argue, and especially the first time, is not to panic. This is not a sign of the end of your romance; in fact, look at it as the opposite. It is a chance for you to express your feelings, clear the air, and learn more about each other and how to communicate. You have the ability to read the non-verbal signs and act upon them accordingly. Arguments also provide a chance for you to learn more about yourself and to take responsibility for your part in the problem instead of blaming your partner. You will both learn how to communicate as a couple, but it's not something that you will just wake up and know how to do. It is something that gets easier and will help you to create a much deeper, meaningful bond.

BUILDING INTIMACY IN A NEW RELATIONSHIP

Back to the fun stuff! Regardless of whether you haven't had sex in a week or a year, the first few months of a relationship should be filled with great sex. You may have been able to step out of your comfort zone and take it out of the bedroom, or even out of the house. It's like being a teenager all over again and you probably have a glow of happiness about you. You might also be starting to feel scared that this honeymoon phase will fizzle out and you will become a couple that only has sex on birthdays and at Christmas.

It is this point that we want to become more intimate. Being intimate and having sex are not the same. Sex isn't necessarily emotional. It can be raw passion, a purely physical act. Let's face it, you don't even have to know someone's name to have sex. Two consenting adults who want to have fun physically without complicating things with feelings can have a one-night stand, it's purely sexual.

Intimacy can involve sex, but there is far more to it than the physical. Being intimate with someone is about a deep emotional connection where you completely trust each other. To be intimate means you can show your vulnerable side and not feel scared.

When you want to be intimate with someone, you will let them see your flabby tummy, even touch it (at least in my case). Intimacy is the cornerstone of a strong, loving relationship. As intimacy requires trust, it takes some time to build both of them up together.

THE NON-PHYSICAL SIDE OF INTIMACY

To build your emotional intimacy, there are plenty of activities you can do that will naturally encourage intimacy to build up:

Share things with your partner. It could be what happened during your day, your dreams and goals in life. The more comfortable you become, the more of your vulnerable side you can begin to share, such as the things you fear or things about the past that you haven't felt ready to talk about yet.

Complement each other. After some time together, you may start to forget to show each other appreciation for the things you do for one another. If he fills your car up with gas, let him know how sweet it was of him. Look him in the eyes and tell him you love him, not because you haven't said it in a while, but because you want to.

Make special time for each other. Once you get settled into your relationship routine, it can seem like everything becomes assumed. You spend plenty of time together but only the usual activities. Keep things fresh by doing something different together. Sign up for a new class or start a new hobby. Make a list of all the new things you would like to try as a couple.

Shake up the routine. If he tends to do all the cooking, dust off your cookbook and try something new. If you are used to breakfast in bed on Sundays, go out for a change. Find a way to inject some of the initial excitement back into your love.

THE PHYSICAL SIDE OF INTIMACY

There are plenty of relationships that have physical intimacy without sex. Don't feel that you can't create a closer connection just because you aren't having sex. Holding hands, an arm around the waist, cuddles on the sofa are all things that couples should do to show their love and affection. Ask them what they like so you know how you can start to feel closer, running your nails down the back of their neck or through their hair. Even things like Eskimo kisses are cute signs of your love.

It is necessary that physical acts of intimacy don't imply a desire for sex. Sometimes, things will naturally progress, but you don't want this to become a habit.

There has to be a clear line between showing your love and wanting sex. If the only affection you show each other is when you want sex, you will never feel love.

THE SEXUAL SIDE OF INTIMACY

Being sexually intimate is still more than just sex. It's about exploring your sexuality together, trying things that haven't had the confidence to do before. Talk about your fantasies and discover ways to be able to fulfil them.

There is no need for you to play a passive role in the bedroom. If you want to have sex, be the one to make the first move. A greater connection will develop when you are both sexually satisfied.

People will still ask me how long the stage of dating takes. How long is a bit of string? As long as you want it to be! You can't put a time frame on this, because each couple is so different. You might be dubious of jumping into something too quickly. You might be enjoying the fun of dating so much that you don't feel the need to push things to move on.

Couples can have their first argument within a month or so; sex can become lovemaking in weeks. There are too many physiological aspects to consider when looking at timeframes for each stage. Be yourself, keep learning about each other inside and outside of the bedroom and your relationship will take its course. Still, there is one other necessary area to cover before we start expecting someone else's love to fill our hearts, and that is the ability to love ourselves. Intimacy will come naturally when communication is open and honest.

There is still something that we must get right before we can even start to entertain the thought of loving someone else. That is, learning to love yourself! It's another fun topic but not one that can be overlooked.

6

LEARNING TO LOVE YOURSELF BEFORE GETTING TO LOVE SOMEONE ELSE

My time in Australia taught me so much about dating. Sadly, it was cut short due to a little visa issue and a very sudden exit out of the country. While that is another story, the long flight home gave me plenty of time for reflection. It was now time to start putting myself first, to focus on my career. I wrote everything in my journal, created my new goals and by the time I landed in the next country, I was determined.

Then it happened again!

My new boss was like something out of a Hugo Boss advert. I still knew that he was out of my league, but this was going to be a major distraction. As the weeks went by, the chemistry grew and despite the adage about not dipping your nib in office ink, I became that girl who was dating the boss.

For whatever reason, he became the only thing that mattered. What he wanted to do, where he wanted to go, the restaurants that we ate in, I agreed with everything, because I couldn't believe that he was interested in me. I would go out of my way to make him happy. I loved him ferociously and was blinded by absolutely everything else. I fell into the trap of being someone's girlfriend instead of being an individual. It didn't mean that he didn't love me. Our relationship lasted for about five years and he is the only ex that I still have a great friendship with. But it was never going to last, because I had no idea who I was, nor did I have a clue how to love myself.

You have probably learnt so much up to this point and you are eager to get out there and start dating. Nevertheless, if you have had a bad relationship, or series of relationships, before you go any further, let's take some time for some introspection. You can't connect with another person until you have created that meaningful connection with yourself.

WHY IS IT IMPORTANT TO LOVE YOURSELF BEFORE LOVING SOMEONE ELSE?

People need love in their lives; it's one of our basic needs, along with food, safety and shelter. We tend to make the assumption that that love has to come from other people, when in fact self-love is just as necessary for our own well-being. To a large extent, it is actually easier to love someone else before ourselves. Self-love requires putting your own needs and wants first and we can often feel like this is a selfish act. Thinking of our loved one first makes us feel like we are good people.

Self-love goes back to your happiness. Can you put your hand on your heart and say that you are happy with your life at this very moment? If there's any hesitation, it strongly suggests that you aren't satisfied with one or several areas of your life. It's hard to admit, but you might be looking for love to make you happy, to bring about that satisfaction you crave. Even though you may have to practice a little patience, it's essential to ensure that you are completely happy in every sense of the word. Let's take a closer look at why self-love has to come first.

Self-love makes it easier to say no

Throughout life, there are always going to be people who ask too much of you; they put themselves first, and can also have a habit of crossing your boundaries or disrespecting your values. Learning to love yourself gives you the power to say "no" to the things that you don't agree with.

Self-love provides time for healing

It's part of your emotional awareness. As you explore the love you have for yourself, you become more in tune with your feelings, both the good and the bad. Allowing yourself to feel pain but then to also feel your love will help you to heal from so much of the bad that has happened to you, and not necessarily just in your love life.

Self-love is necessary to learn more about yourself

As you are taking a good look at yourself, you begin to appreciate more about your likes and dislikes, what makes you buzz with excitement and what makes you so angry you could cry. Self-love helps you to understand more about the real you and what you want, not what you thought you have wanted that would make others happy.

Your confidence will start to grow

Loving yourself because you are beautiful, kind, and intelligent is such a warming and fulfilling sense. When you see that you don't have to change and you really are an amazing person, you can feel your confidence grow and you stop looking for approval from others. The need to hear the words "I love you" is replaced with a want to hear the words. The difference is subtle, but it is most definitely there.

You become better at making decisions

As your confidence starts to grow and your self-love encourages you to put your own needs first, the decisions you make from this point are smarter. Instead of making choices based on the best outcome for others, you think about options that make everyone happy.

You learn to forgive

If a past relationship went wrong, you would have had a part in this and so would the other person. Self-love lets you dig deep into the grudges you hold and those negative emotions that are hard to let go of. It allows you forgive yourself for the mistakes you make, and this makes it easier to forgive the other person.

. . .

Loving yourself lets you feel worthy of love

If you don't love yourself, it is hard to imagine that you deserve love from others.

When you start to feel that love inside of you, then you will be ready to share it. Without it, you could end up sharing something you think is love but that isn't the real thing, i.e., doing their washing and cooking as a sign of love.

We mustn't get self-love confused with being selfish. Being selfish is always putting yourself before others. Self-love is about knowing when your needs should come first by being aware of your emotions. Say, for example, your partner wants to have dinner with his or her family, but you never agree. This is being selfish, because you always consider your own happiness before theirs. Now let's say that you have been to the in-laws for the last four Sunday dinners, but this weekend, you really need a day at home to catch up on other things. This is self-love.

HOW CAN YOU TELL IF YOU LOVE YOURSELF?

It's a little more than looking in the mirror, giving yourself that motivational wink and saying "I love you". Self-love incorporates everything from how you take care of yourself to your authenticity. See how you answer the following questions to determine if you are on the right track or if you need a bit of a self-love makeover.

Do you have strong connections with friends and family?

Self-love is a powerful magnet that attracts others to you and makes your relationships stronger.

Do you celebrate your wins?

Those who celebrate all of their successes, both big and small, have more motivation and confidence to handle the bigger challenges in life.

Do you celebrate other people's wins?

If you are truly happy with yourself and your life, you should be able to be happy for the successes of others and not to feel envious.

Are you assertive?

Those who love themselves know what they want but they also know how to go about getting it in a way that doesn't upset others.

Is there direction in your life?

Self-love means you are more self-aware. So, you have your goals and you have a plan to achieve them.

Can you proudly express your emotions?

I cry at MasterChef Kids and I don't hide it and I often laugh at things that really aren't that funny, but it feels good to express my emotions and I prefer this to bottling them up.

Are you in touch with your instincts?

When you can follow your instincts, it means that you trust the judgements and decisions you make.

Can you be yourself?

Being yourself goes beyond speaking your mind. You should be able to wear what you want to instead of following the latest trends because that is what is expected.

Do you take care of your body?

When your body tells you it's tired, you should listen and get more rest. You should have a healthier diet and get the right amount of exercise.

Have you let go of toxic relationships?

People who continuously let you down or hurt you do not respect you. Loving yourself means you are aware of those who don't treat you right and put distance between them.

Are you grateful for your life?

It's too easy to take things for granted and not appreciate everything that is available to us.

Have you stopped the negative self-talk?

So, when you do look in the mirror, you have to be able to see the good and not the bad. Though no one is perfect, self-criticism will not help to promote self-love.

Don't get me wrong, self-love doesn't mean that life is rosy and there are no problems. It's our mentality and how we handle those problems that point to our self-love. A couple of years ago, I had a string of problems and each one seemed to get bigger and bigger. Waking up to the feeling of "not this again" is an exhausting way to live. We get the "why me?" sensations and "what have I done to deserve this?"

By learning how to love myself, I changed my mentality. I had to start off taking baby steps, so it wasn't a case of waking up one morning with a new outlook on life. Some people take just a week or so to learn how to love themselves, others take a little longer. There is no race and like everything we are learning in this book, it's about enjoying the process!

LEARNING HOW TO LOVE YOURSELF

The first step is to remind yourself that self-love is a wonderful thing that is necessary for us to be able to live a more fulfilling life where we can reach our potential, have fun, and create some incredible relationships along the way.

1. Make changes to your lifestyle

You don't need to go on a diet, throw all the chocolate out and join a gym. Just make a few changes that will start to make you physically feel better. Be strict about getting plenty of water and cut down on things like caffeine and alcohol. If you are anything like me and a bit of a fussy eater, you can try to experiment with different foods to keep a balanced diet.

2. Discover what you are good at

It's time to start focusing on your strengths and recognise your skills. Each of us has a talent that the next person doesn't, and you should find confidence in this. It should also give you a sense of pride, especially as you start to share these skills with others.

3. Stop the self-talk—no excuses

You may need to find a trick so that you can be firmer about this. Instead of the traditional 'swear pot', have a 'negative pot'. Every negative thought about yourself is going to cost you from this day on. Negative beliefs about ourselves don't only impact the ability to self-love. When we repeat what we consider our failures to other people, they start to believe them too.

4. Use the negative pot to encourage positive thoughts

As you banish the negative thoughts, start to replace them with positive beliefs about yourself. Each time you add a coin to your pot, think of something positive. You don't need to go around shouting these great things to the world, but you do need to believe them. If you find it hard, and this is perfectly normal, write down a list and keep adding to it.

5. Don't feel you have to be perfect

It's ok to lose your temper or not to know how to explain your feelings. Sometimes you will get things wrong, because nobody is perfect. When you start to let go of perfectionism, it becomes easier to see all of the amazing things about yourself.

6. Say no when you want to

It might be one of the most challenging steps to take, because we have this mentality that saying no to others is narcissistic or selfish. Every time somebody asks something of you, take some time to think whether you can and whether you want to do it. If the request feels like it will take too much from you, learn how to say no in a firm but polite way. Asserting yourself doesn't make you a bad person.

7. Look closely at your group of friends

When you start putting yourself first and saying no to those around you, you may get some resistance. This could be people disrespecting your 'no' or not appreciating your thoughts and values. Decide for yourself if these people are really the friends you want in your life or whether they are dragging you down.

8. Listen to your feelings

When you stub your toe, while you are cursing, your body is sending numerous messages. Our feelings also send several different messages. When you learn how to listen to these emotional messages you can learn if you are doing right by your body.

9. Find your energy

For me, apart from taking care of my health, I find my energy when I am motivated and inspired. This energy helps me to get more done, tick off things on the to-do list and reach my goals. The vicious negative circle has been replaced with a positive flow.

10. Remember that it can always be far worse!

Did you know that 15% of the human population was born with a physical or mental disability? Global hunger affects 8.9% of people, and 20% of the world lacks adequate housing. This doesn't mean that you don't have the right to complain every now and again; we need to get things off our chest and I'm certainly not belittling anyone's problems. Try to make your complaining constructive and remember that no matter what, things could still be worse.

WHAT TO DO WHEN SELF-LOVE IS CHALLENGED BY THE MISTAKES WE MAKE

How strongly we berate ourselves when we make a mistake! You miss something off the shopping list (normally the only thing you actually needed) and you are the world's worst human. Or you miss a meeting, forget your kid has a bake sale on at school... whatever mistake women make, we punish ourselves ten times over. We think we should have known better or that it was a stupid thing to have done.

When you are trying to learn how to love yourself, making mistakes can be a real knock to your confidence and even put you back a step or two. It becomes harder to see the good and those negative beliefs start to fill our minds. Even when we talk about our mistakes, it is always with a negative tone when really, we should be paying more attention to the lesson that can be learnt.

Let's say you see a dating profile that you like, but there is one thing about it that you don't like. Your gut tells you not to meet, but you do anyway. You later see the mistake you made and start to call yourself an idiot. What you should be doing is patting your instincts on the back and remembering to listen in the future, because honestly, you aren't an idiot.

At the end of the day, because we have accepted that we aren't perfect, we also need to accept the fact that we will make mistakes in life. I bet you can't name one person who, since the day they were born, hasn't made a mistake. So, the first thing to remember is that you are not alone.

Take just a moment to think how bad the mistake really was and what the worst-case scenario could be. Regardless of gender, we tend to blow things out of proportion on occasions. In the case of the bad date, the worst thing is that you spent a night on a date when you could have been doing something else. If you make a mistake at work, you say sorry, you take responsibility for the mistake and you move on, knowing what not to do the next time. If you are sitting down reading this book, it means that no mistake you have ever made led to the end of the world.

Another good way to stop beating yourself up about making mistakes is to bear in mind that only people who are doing things make mistakes. If you are sitting on your sofa day in and day out, of course you aren't going to do anything wrong—you aren't living. As long as you are living your life and working towards your goals, you will make mistakes. Looking at it this way makes it seem quite sad not to make them.

When you make a mistake, accept it, admit to it, apologise if you have to. This is what others will respect in you. Learn from it so that you don't do it again. Remind yourself of the things you did well in the situation. Then put it behind you. Dwelling on it will only cause you to start doubting yourself and at this point, nothing can be done to turn back time, so stop hurting yourself more.

Self-love may have a bit of a hippy ring to it and that is because the concept first came about in the late `50s or early `60s. But that is not to say by learning to love yourself, you are going to transform into a flower child. Self-awareness sounds more "psychological" and "professional" but really, they are both about understanding yourself, your feelings, and your actions. Self-love takes it a little further by acting on those feelings so that you are able to live happily. You might not master it straight away and it may not hit you in the face all of a sudden, but over time, you will begin to see the positive impacts of loving yourself and then you will know you are ready to love someone else and to embrace their love.

7

WHY YOU SHOULD NEVER PUT YOUR HAPPINESS IN SOMEBODY ELSE'S HANDS

I t might have been you or you may have heard it from other women, but how do you feel when you hear things like "he completes me", "my better half" or "he is the Yin to my Yang"? We know what someone is trying to say, that they are truly, madly, and deeply in love with their soulmate. But let's examine these popular expressions closer.

When you are struggling through one bad date after another, all you really want is to find that person who completes you or creates that balance that you have been looking for. I know I did. I thought that this was the sign of a strong relationship. As I got older, I understood the fatal mistake of needing someone to complete me. This meant that I wasn't happy with who I was. To put it simply, it's like going out without your bra. It's probably only you that knows it's missing, but without it, your outfit isn't complete. Would you go and ask a stranger to offer you some support under your top? No! You can't ask your partner to provide whatever it is you are missing to make you feel complete.

When I went through a stage of empowering myself, I thought a lot about the whole Yin and Yang and I loved the idea of two people joining as if to complete a puzzle, but there was still a niggling feeling that I should have been able to complete my own puzzle. I felt like if I didn't have everything to make myself happy, any love between myself and my partner would be like pouring water into a bucket with a hole in it. A decent amount was going to escape.

There are multiple reasons why we might not be happy. We may still be hurting from a previous relationship; we might be suffering from trauma or grief. For so many of us, we aren't happy with our appearance, or even our careers. But regardless of why we are unhappy, it is up to us to put it right. Taking responsibility for our feelings means the good and the bad.

WHY IT IS ESSENTIAL THAT YOU TAKE RESPONSIBILITY FOR YOUR OWN HAPPINESS

Only you know what can make you happy

I love how when you ask someone what makes them angry, they can probably list anywhere between five and ten things—queues, traffic, in-laws, chewing with your mouth open etc. But when it comes to listing what makes us happy, we have to think a little more carefully, unless of course we just list what we think people want to hear.

What makes you happy will vary from day to day; a hug from your loved one might do the trick on a Monday but by Friday it could be a night out with friends. There are the smaller things in life, like a nice meal, or the general things, like the holiday you have been saving up for. Suppose you are struggling to understand what makes you happy. In that case, it's going to be pretty impossible for somebody else to do it for you.

It's not fair to put the responsibility on someone else

When your partner feels like your happiness is their responsibility, there is an awful lot of pressure put on them. They too have their own feelings and actions that they have to manage. If you know how hard it is to control your own happiness, you can only imagine being responsible for somebody else's too.

Someone who is tasked with making you feel happy will be taking essential time away from themselves, which in turn could lead them to resent you. That's certainly not what we are looking for in a relationship. It may even get to the point that they are walking on eggshells, trying to please you. Speaking of eggs…

You have put all of your eggs in one basket

Let's say that you are in a relationship and this person makes you happy. The effort they have to put into the relationship for it to work is far greater than yours. They will soon become tired of this. You have become dependent on another person, which is incredibly unhealthy.

If this is the only thing in your life that is making you happy, when it comes to an end, you are going to be left devastated and broken. The healing process is going to be harder and probably take longer. You are likely going to have to start rediscovering yourself all over again. Your happiness has to come from more than just one person.

You have handed over the power

It's not always the case, but there will be some people who will be able to manipulate you because they know they have power over you. As they are the ones making you happy and now you are dependent on that person, their wish is pretty much your command.

Because you feel that you need this person, you will do anything not to risk losing them. If they want to move to a new house, you have to go along. If they want or don't want children, you won't wish to rock the boat. Not only have you handed this person the keys to your heart, but also to your life.

You will always be looking for more

We have this habit of thinking that the next stage of a relationship is going to bring us more happiness, but this is going to bring about unrealistic expectations. When you are dating, you can't wait for things to get more serious, then you can only imagine how happy you will be living with this person. Marriage must bring about a new sense of security that will provide the ultimate happiness.

It's a bit like a dog chasing its tail. You keep looking for something that you may not find, because you are looking in the wrong place. For many, this realisation comes too late, and they are already married with children. The risk here is that you have to learn what makes you happy and it may turn out to not be the person you are with.

You could become a 'serial dater'

Dating different people at the same time gives you the chance to explore different potential partners and learn more about each other. This is a good thing, even great. But serial dating is jumping from one relationship to the next without understanding what you really want, or what will make you happy.

If you notice that you have had a series of dates and nothing is going right, it often means you are dating the wrong type of people. You are looking for those who will make you happy instead of someone you can be happy with. It's time to take a step back and dedicate some time to introspection.

You might be slightly confused at this point. Obviously, we want a happy relationship and it is only logical that we look for a partner who is going to make us feel happy. Imagine a dating profile that said, "I'm looking for someone who will annoy me and make me angry". The problem is when we need that person to make us happy. So many of us get things the wrong way around and start dating when we aren't happy. When your dates and relationships go wrong, you look for every possible reason and the reason is most likely under your nose.

It's not uncommon to be oblivious to our own happiness. In a world where life is often extremely sad and challenging, and in which we are taught to focus on the happiness of others, sometimes I could go for months without even considering my happiness. When was the last time you asked yourself if you were genuinely happy?

REASONS WHY WE DON'T LOOK FOR OUR OWN HAPPINESS

Apart from feeling selfish, searching for our own happiness can make us step out of our comfort zone and make us feel uneasy. There is so much going on in our brain, including things we aren't consciously aware of, that we probably have never thought about the following reasons. I know the first time I learnt about them, I was in complete denial. You too might read the following and tut away saying "That's not me", but these reasons are often aimed at your inner self, rather than the logical part of you who is reading this.

Not going after what we want in life challenges the way we see ourselves. Your personality has been forming since before you could walk and you are probably now comfortable with the way you see yourself, even if you aren't happy. Your inner self doesn't want to be disturbed. Wanting to change not only disturbs our inner self but it also kicks it into action, and we start to criticise ourselves for wanting something better.

At the same time as our personality was developing, so were our defences. We have built a solid wall around us that protects us from getting hurt. Those defences that we built up are going to be counterproductive in adult life. For example, if you want to be loved but have built a wall up so that you can't get hurt, you aren't going to ever be able to experience true love. It's only when we gently let our guard down that we can start to experience happiness, but this comes at a risk, and Ms Inner Self is not happy about this risk.

We just wouldn't be who we are without feeling guilty for absolutely everything we do! From the bar of chocolate to saying no to Mum, we feel terrible! Wanting the things in life that make us feel happy can cause us to feel guilty because we are putting ourselves first and to an extent, we may be leaving others behind us. Suppose you want a promotion at work and you know this will mean you are earning more than your partner. In that case, it can seem like you are ahead of the metaphorical game and you may feel guilty about this, more so if they have been stuck in the same position for a while. This guilt can be strong enough for some women not to take that promotion.

Finally, finding what makes us happy can stir up old memories and we need to face the pain this creates. Getting married to the right person opened some old relationship wounds which forced me to think about the time I had spent not getting what I wanted. Nobody wants to look back at the past and regret certain choices, but don't be surprised if there are moments of pain when you reach that moment of happiness.

WHAT IS INTROSPECTION?

To say that introspection is a way of exploring your mental state of mind, your thoughts and feelings, is a little insulting considering its complexity and over forty years of research. Wilhelm Wundt, the father of experimental psychology, developed the technique of introspection during the late 1800s. He used it to help others to understand their thought processes objectively and to understand how events in the past related to experiences today. It was seen as a structure to learn how certain things affected people in different ways.

Today, we see introspection as a less formal concept, one that gives us a chance to look closer at who we are and learn more about ourselves. Introspection is synonymous with self-examination and self-reflection. When you consider that 90% of the approximately 50,000 daily thoughts we have are negative, introspection is essential for personal growth.

Getting Introspection Right

It's not as simple as just thinking why something made you angry while you are out getting your groceries, although this is still better than just pushing the feeling back down. Introspection involves asking some difficult questions and thinking before responding. You will need to take some time and space for yourself, so first make sure you are in a quiet area and you aren't in any kind of rush.

Here are fifteen questions to ask yourself and it's ok if one question leads you to another. They are just some ideas that will help you to get started.

1. Do I have a healthy, positive outlook on life?
2. Am I thinking negatively before I go to sleep?
3. Do I get stressed by things that are out of my control?
4. Am I true to myself?
5. Am I looking after my physical and emotional self?
6. Why do I matter?
7. What matters in my life?

8. What is my purpose in life?
9. Am I doing everything possible to achieve my purpose?
10. Am I challenging myself?
11. What am I really scared of?
12. Do I make the most of my time?
13. Are there things in life I take for granted?
14. How have I been kind today?
15. Who can I trust in life?
16. What do I love about life?
17. What are twenty things that make me smile?
18. What is enough for me?
19. What do I want to learn?
20. Which ten words best describe me?

When you start to answer these questions, don't judge yourself. You aren't being interviewed for Miss America, so if world peace isn't the first thing that matters in your life, don't feel like a terrible person. Also, remember to dig deep, even if the answers scare you. It's a given that you are scared of spiders or heights, but what fears do you have that are so strong you don't even tell anyone else? If you feel it helps, write your answers down.

Once you have started looking into these questions, you might want to start asking some that are more open-ended. Every now and again I like to ask myself some of the following questions and make a note to see how my thoughts and feelings change over time:

- If I had a whole day to myself, I would…
- If there was one thing I couldn't live without, it would be…
- The one piece of advice I would give my teenage self is…
- I am most satisfied when I am…
- I feel loved when…

For a bit of introspection every day, keeping a journal is an excellent tool. Take a few minutes to write down one positive event and one positive thought or emotion you have. Also, look at what you have done that day to bring you closer to your goals and choose one question for yourself. It could be one of the questions we have mentioned above or one that has stemmed from a previous question. You shouldn't answer this question immediately. Take the next day to reflect on it and consider it in more depth. The next day you can answer the question and write the next one.

Introspection can be scary, particularly if you don't have a great deal of self-esteem or confidence. Don't be scared to face your fears. It is an enlightening experience and when you start to focus on the good things, you will feel your confidence grow. More than anything, you will learn more about yourself than you could have thought possible and you will probably find a lot of weight lifted off of your shoulders and an extra spring in your step.

FINDING YOUR HAPPINESS FIRST

Ok, so first things first, well done! The scary part is over. You have taken that long hard look at yourself and it is time to find your happiness. Never forget that finding and putting your own happiness first is not selfish: it's your right as a human being and nobody else is going to do it for you. You wouldn't feel guilty or selfish for doing the housework because nobody else wants to do it! If you haven't discovered what makes you happy yet, here are some more ideas.

Analyse your days

I took a week to make a note of all the things I did in one week and put them into three categories, 'happy', 'unhappy' and '50/50'. You have to be brutally honest. Initially, I put shopping in 50/50 because it is something that you kind of just have to do. But really, it made me unhappy. At the end of the week, I had a clear picture of the number of things that made me happy compared to those that didn't. I found this a useful process for the next step.

Decide if the situation or your mentality needs to change

While we are on the topic of housework, it's Saturday morning, the sun is shining but your house is a disaster. You have to clean before you can do anything else. We can't change this situation, except for leaving it for the next day, but how much is that really going to help? You can look at your housework as a horrible way to spend your Saturday and you can complain about every step...

Or you can change your mentality. The great thing about cleaning is the end result. It's sitting down and everything is looking and smelling fresher. It's getting rid of the weekly collection of rubbish and throwing it all out, which helps me feel calmer. It's taking pride in your home. Pour a large coffee, write down the chores, pick your favourite playlist and have some fun.

There are so many things for which you need to decide where the change lies. For some people, a career change isn't possible, so it will have to be a change in mentality so that you can enjoy your work more. You might find that your weekly gym session does fill you with the same energy as it used to, which is something you can easily change.

Take responsibility for your happiness

I know it's been said before, but you can't be passive with regards to your own happiness. You have to choose to be happy actively. You might need some help to remind you of this. Think of using Post-It notes or start your day with affirmations like "I am happy". There will still be times when you feel sad or angry. It's up to you to change those negative emotions back into happiness so that they don't fester.

Stay away from negatives

I refuse to watch the news, because it is so horrendously negative. I'm sure when I was a kid, they always used to finish with a positive or happy story! It's not that I'm not concerned about what happens in the world. But I have an app and choose to read the news when I know I am in a good mental place, so it doesn't bring me down. I won't accept complainers. You know those types of people who at first you make such an effort to cheer them up, only to realise that it's in their blood. Unfortunately, you might not be able to remove them from your life completely, but you can choose not to listen to the negativity.

Be comfortable alone

Can you sit on the sofa for an evening and not feel lonely? What about booking a table for one at a restaurant? If you are still feeling sad when you spend time by yourself, it indicates that you aren't whole, that you are still missing something to complete you. It is time to start finding out why you don't like being alone. Some people think it is a sign that this is their destiny. Others get nervous and agitated because they have nobody to talk to. Not wanting to eat alone in a restaurant is usually from fear of what others think of you. Start looking at new hobbies that will make you happy. Joining a class is a good way to remain social but also something that you can do alone.

Break away from dependence

When you date or your partner is late, you might find yourself waiting and like a boiling kettle, just getting angrier and angrier. It is essential that you break away from this type of behaviour. You can't need someone that much and it's not fair on yourself. The best way to do it is to carry on with your plans regardless of whether they have made it or not. If you have planned to go to the cinema, go. Or if you were invited to a party, go. They will be missing out, not you. Also, you have the opportunity to be happy rather than sitting there fuming, potentially leading to an argument.

Stay focused on your goals and your health

Make an effort to eat a healthy, balanced diet. If you aren't big on exercise, at least walk. Get out into nature and enjoy some fresh air. This will help you sleep and when you are well-rested, it is much easier to be happy. Practice mindfulness and meditation so that you can bring some peace to your mind.

Continuously reassess your goals, both the long-term and the short-term. Make sure they are realistic, and that you have a plan to achieve them. Like happiness, you have to own your goals and you must take responsibility for them. Relying on others is the fastest way to experience setbacks.

Spoil yourself

When you get caught up in life, the days can pass by with the same routine, the same ups and downs and we don't celebrate just being. Give yourself a five-minute face mask or get on Amazon and buy whatever it is you have been wanting but putting off in case something more important comes up. It doesn't have to be anything huge or expensive. It doesn't even have to be for you. Send your mum some flowers for no reason other than that it makes you happy.

. . .

Be financially wise and financially independent

This one is a biggy! Not having money to do the things that make you happy is simply horrible. The stress of having financial difficulties makes it incredibly difficult to see any joy in life. Create a budget and be strict about sticking to it. Make sure everything gets paid off first.

Never depend on a partner for money, otherwise you are handing them the power. It's normal that when things get serious you might want to have a joint account to pay the bills, but you pay in equally and keep your separate personal account for you to spend as you wish. Being financially independent will take a great strain off your relationship. This is sometimes difficult if you are responsible for the home rather than in paid employment. Although it sounds a bit official or formal, it is worth having an open conversation about this and coming to an agreement.

Find things that make you laugh

It sounds a bit obvious, but don't wait until something happens that makes you smile and laugh. Go out and find it. Search for some funny videos and save them for emergencies. When you feel a little down, go to your funny space for an instant cheer-me-up. Being a nice person makes me smile, like talking to old people. On a similar note, be a kind person. Compassion, kindness and positivity are contagious.

Ironically, it's quite sad to think how difficult it is to put our own happiness first. When I first started delving into my own happiness, I was taken back by my findings. I thought I was happy. I thought I knew what I liked and what I didn't, but really, I noticed that too much of my time was spent making other people happy and assuming that this was what was making me happy. What I wanted and needed had become lost.

It's hard to take that close look at yourself. You might feel like you have opened Pandora's box and you just aren't sure what you are going to find. The harsh reality is, you may not like what you find. On the other hand, once you are there, you can also see all of the beauty within you. It's a reminder of all of your skills and abilities and all that you are capable of achieving.

If you are not happy with yourself, you can't expect someone else to be. If you need someone else to make you complete or happy, you might find that the dynamics of the relationship are out of place. Only when you are truly happy will you be able to find a person who you can be happy with. You will be able to build a strong, more honest relationship where you can feel confident in asserting yourself. You won't feel selfish about taking care of yourself first. The journey to finding your own happiness will lead you to independence and confidence.

CONCLUSION

We have covered it all, from learning what love is for you to how far you should go on your first date. We have pulled back all of the layers and discovered the person that we really are and now we are ready to show the world.

You might have begun some of the practices in this book as you were going along, or you might have waited to learn everything before starting this amazing and fun journey of dating in the modern world. The first place to start is with yourself. It's about taking the time to understand what matters to you and where you want to see yourself in the next week, month, year, etc. Before even thinking about creating an online dating profile, it is essential to look in the mirror and be happy with what you see.

If your emotions are all over the place and you are feeling unsettled in your world, you need to learn how to find some peace and to slow things down. Analyse your relationships, not only romantic ones but also those with your friends and family. While you are exploring yourself, your feelings, and your connections to the world, don't focus on the negatives. Everything that has happened in your life up to now has led you to this moment, and we should learn from the good and the bad and rid ourselves of the assumption that this is how life is set to be. You have the control and you can make all of the necessary changes, whether physical or mental.

Once you feel settled within yourself and you know how to live a happy and fulfilling life without the need for anyone to fill in any gaps, you know you will be ready to start dating again. Don't forget the importance of self-love, even before you begin dating. Self-love and happiness are the foundations of a successful relationship.

Don't be sucked into what society tells us. The world is slowly catching up to modern ways, but we are still going to come across people who believe that women aren't supposed to go out there and get what they want. Prince Charming is not going to knock on our door and whisk us away. We need to stop looking for our hero and become our own heroine. More to the point, if we are happy and independent, we simply don't need to be rescued!

Successful dating is about knowing what your purpose is and this goes back to modern dating. You can be any age and decide that you want to date just to have fun. You may not want a commitment and all you are looking for is someone to enjoy life with. And yes, maybe you just want sex. Knowing this and being comfortable with it is empowering and don't feel ashamed of it in any way. Sex is great exercise and far more fun than going to the gym! Also, don't be surprised if some men are taken back if you tell them that you are only looking for sex; we still have to work on teaching men that not every woman wants to get married and become a mother to their children. When you clearly tell someone what your purpose is, it takes a lot of pressure off the experience and it removes false expectations.

Creating your online profile isn't always a walk in the park. However, if you have taken the necessary steps to learn about yourself and what makes you happy, it is much easier. You will have the confidence to list your positives and from the first moment, prospective dates will see the real you that isn't hiding behind what you think people want to see.

Please don't forget the safety tips on creating an online dating profile. Never give out any personal details or financial information, and don't include photos of identifiable locations. Online dating is a great, straightforward way to meet people, but not everyone out there is honest. As long as you are sensible and follow your instincts, you will be able to have a safe and enjoyable experience.

The same safety must be taken when chatting to people online and meeting them. Don't feel any pressure into handing out information that you don't want to give. You will know when it feels right to give someone your phone number. If someone is too insistent, it might be for the wrong reasons. It is also a sign that they don't respect your boundaries, something you may continue to have problems with later on. Meet dates in a public place and always tell someone where you are going and who you are with. The chances are absolutely nothing will go wrong, but in online dating, the rule of thumb is that it's better to be safe than sorry.

Those first few dates are such a wonderful experience, regardless of the outcome. You are living! You are meeting new people and learning new things. Excitement is running wild and you feel youthful and energized. Even if you are in your twenties, it's still great to feel like you are sixteen again! Mistakes will be made;

don't punish yourself for this. Learn and move on and remember you are lucky to have stories to tell. Try not to date just one person. You run the risk of falling in love too soon and being blind to their flaws. Meeting a few people allows you to decide on the things that you can see past and the things that you can't imagine living with. As long as you are honest with your dates, you aren't doing anything wrong. And, as long as you are enjoying yourself while you are dating, you aren't wasting any time.

Turning your dates into a relationship should come about naturally. You should start to feel comfortable talking about more serious topics and you will be able to learn more about what you both want from life. Your values should be clear by now, as should your boundaries. There should be a warm feeling between you, one that sees you both relaxed to show each other the more intimate sides.

And ending on a high, don't let anyone tell you when the right time to have sex is. It's a decision between two consenting adults, not society. If it's on the first date, good for you, if it's after a few weeks or months, that's great. If you feel nervous about having sex, tell your date or your partner this. They should have respect for your feelings and find ways to help you feel more relaxed. Don't forget that men too can feel nervous and even if your hormones are raging, you need to respect their feelings too. Trust yourself to know when it's right and you know what I'm going to say next—be safe!

I have had so much fun writing this book and although I made tons of mistakes while I was dating, I have reached a place where I can look back and remember all the good times that I had too. It has been a reminder that even when we are happily married, we need to continue working on our own happiness to ensure the relationship stays healthy. If you have enjoyed reading this book, I would love to hear your opinions and stories in a quick Amazon review. Reviews are the best way that we can help other ladies break free from unhappy ineffective dating and start enjoying their lives too.

Thank you for reading my book. If you have enjoyed reading it perhaps you would like to leave a star rating and a review for me on Amazon? It really helps support writers like myself create more books. You can leave a review for me by scanning the QR code below:

Thank you so much. Joanna Wells

REFERENCES

4 Huge Mistakes Guys Make in Their Online Dating Profiles. (n.d.). Retrieved from https://www. menaskem.com/ four-online-dating-profile-mistakes

33% of Couples Met Online. (2016, March 16). Retrieved from https://www.confetti.co.uk/wedding/ news/33- percent-of-couples-met-online/

Beck, J. (2020, February 14). How Do You Know If You're Ready for a Relationship? Retrieved from https://www.theatlantic.com/family/archive/2019/05/ how-do-   you-know-if-youre-ready-for-a-relationship/588871/

Brown, D. (2011, June 9). 15% worldwide have physical or mental disability. Retrieved from https://www.

cbsnews.com/news/15-worldwide-have-physical -or-mental-disability/

Buffalmano, L. (2020, May 15). 7 Biggest Early Dating Mistakes Women Do (With Pics & Solutions) | TPM. Retrieved from https://thepowermoves.com/women-biggest-dating-mistakes/

Carter, H. (2019, January 9). The Grown Woman's Guide to Online Dating. Retrieved from https://www.oprahmag.com/ life/relationships-love/a25776713/guide-to-online-dating/

Chamie, J. (2017, July 13). As Cities Grow, So Do the Numbers of Homeless | YaleGlobal Online. Retrieved from https://yaleglobal.yale.edu/content/cities-grow-so-do- numbers-homeless

Eharmony. (n.d.). Retrieved from https://www.eharmony.com/dating-advice/about-you/eight- signs-you-may-not-be-ready-for-a-relationship/

Firestone, L. (2015, July 15). 5 Reasons We Don't Let Ourselves Be Happy. Retrieved from https://www.psychologytoday.com/us/blog/compassion-matters/201507/5-reasons-we-dont-let-ourselves-be-happy

George, A. (2019, March 28). 10 Reasons Why Self-Love Is The Best, Most Important Type Of Love. Retrieved from https://www.yourtango.com/

2019322014/reasons-why- self-love-best-type-of-love-yourself-first

Herrin, T. (2019, June 1). What Is Introspection? Psychology, Definition, And Applications | Betterhelp. Retrieved from https://www.betterhelp.com/advice/ psychologists/what-is-introspection-psychology-definition -and-applications/

Jolly, B. (2019, April 30). Sex on first date is "IMPORTANT if you want a serious relationship." Retrieved from https://www.mirror.co.uk/news/uk-news/sex-first-date-important -you-14975753

Naim, R. (2019, October 14). 40 Signs You've Finally Learned To Love Yourself. Retrieved from https:// thoughtcatalog.com/rania-naim/2016/04/40-sings-youve -finally-learned-to-love-yourself/

Ohlin, B. (2020, September 1). 7 Ways to Improve Communication in Relationships [Update 2019]. Retrieved from https://positivepsychology.com/ communication-in -relationships/

Robinson, L. (2019, June). Dating Tips for Finding the Right Person - HelpGuide.org. Retrieved from https:// www.helpguide.org/articles/relationships-communication /tips-for-finding-lasting-love.htm

Tartakovsky, M. (2018, October 10). Why Healthy Relationships Always Have Boundaries & How to Set Boundaries in Yours. Retrieved from https://psychcentral.com/blog/why-healthy-relationships-always-have-boundaries-how-to-set-boundaries-in-yours/

Toglia, M. (2018, June 5). How To Figure Out What You Want In A Partner — And Feel Confident Asking For It. Retrieved from https://www.bustle.com/p/how-to-figure- out-what-you-want-in-a-partner-feel-confident-asking- for-it-9168822

Walster, E. (n.d.). "Playing hard to get": Understanding an elusive phenomenon. Retrieved from https://psycnet.apa.org/record/1973-24846-001

Wilson, R. E. (2015, December 14). Loving Yourself: a How-to Guide. Retrieved from https://www.psychologytoday.com/us/blog/the-main-ingredient/201512/loving-yourself-how-guide

Worland, C. (2019, May 1). Your Happiness is Your Own Responsibility: Learn How to Obtain It. Retrieved from https://girlseekingpurpose.com/happiness-is-your -responsibility/

World Hunger: Key Facts and Statistics 2020. (2020, July 15). Retrieved from https://www.actionagainsthunger.org/ world-hunger-facts-statistics

Printed in Great Britain
by Amazon